THE
MESSAGING
CONNECTION

How to Increase Profits by Connecting With People the Way They Want

RYAN J CHAPMAN

Published by RJC Publishing
220 N 1300 W Ste 4, Pleasant Grove, UT 84062

Ryan J Chapman
220 N 1300 W Ste 4, Pleasant Grove, UT 84062
(949) 835-5300

Printed in the United States of America

Dedication:

Special thanks to my daughter Sarah and my Mom for their countless hours of research, preparation and editing.

To Trent for being the business partner anyone would be lucky to have.

To my wife for her constant support and unwavering belief in me.

To every small business owner who has the courage to enter the game and play all out.

CONTENTS

WARNING

Ultimately, this book will teach you how to connect with people in a mobile world and as a result increase your bottom line profits, BUT...

Like anything in life, to get to a solid understanding of how to do something better, you've first got to go deep before you can go up.

Start with the introduction. It's not optional. It sets the stage for everything else.

Then take each chapter in turn. Don't be tempted to skip ahead to the **good stuff**.

This book was carefully written to lead you on a journey that will change the way you see the world, exposing you to latent opportunities that have been hidden to you thus far.

I've done my very best to cut out any fluff without making this book a boring manual.

Introduction

A DRAMATIC SHIFT

There is a saying…

The map is not the territory.

It means our perception of facts is not the same as the facts. Yet there is a natural tendency to forget that our map is just that...a map. We instead slip into the assumption that our map IS the territory.

Assuming the map is the territory can be very dangerous to our chances of discovering and taking advantage of big opportunities. Especially opportunities that have developed since our map was last updated.

I have a 2009 Honda Pilot that has a built in navigation system. But there is one problem: the maps are from 2009.

Where I live they have added a number of important roads that make getting around much easier since 2009.

If my kids, who drive the car, were to plug in an address, there is a very good chance that the route will take much longer because of the missing roads.

Sometimes, the destination doesn't even exist on the map because the roads had not been built in 2009. If they relied on the Pilot's map, they wouldn't even be able to get home!

Can you imagine how difficult it would be to build your business if you were running off of maps from 2009 in today's world?

And yet, for many that is the case.

The territory has changed dramatically in the last few years, but most of the business owners I meet are still working with maps last updated in 2005.

This book is a map update. It is a combination of trends and principles. The trends will continue to evolve and as a result you'll need to know what trends to watch. This book will help you do that.

Principles are timeless, but are also dynamic. This book will update your principles as well. Principles are more valuable than trends, because in large part, principles anticipate trends. They represent some very clear land marks of the territory that the human race has mapped out better than others.

Over the course of your life, if you want bigger and better opportunities, you've got to improve your map so that it better represents the territory.

Fortunately, territory changes happen over time. They are not instant. They unfold slowly. But if you're watching for them, you'll see them immediately.

The central territory change that concerns us now started in the 90s, but really began to bloom in 2007. Then during the 4th quarter of 2011 something so dramatic, so monumental, occurred, that it has earned the beginning of this book.

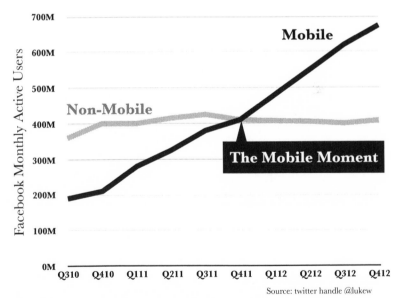

Source: twitter handle @lukew

For the first time, Facebook's mobile monthly active users exceeded non-mobile traffic.

In some developing countries, Facebook IS the internet. But even in the United States, in 2011, Facebook dominated a large majority of internet consumption time.

Facebook's **Mobile Moment**, a phrase popularized by Luke Wroblewski (*check out his twitter feed at @lukew*), is significant because it is a sign that most of the time your potential customers are spending online is now happening on a smart phone screen.

If you were born before 1985 there is a good chance that most of your formative internet experience happened on the computer screen.

That experience formed your map and is now impacting many of your business decisions.

To you, the internet is probably something you think about in terms of a computer first and a smartphone second. But increasingly folks are ONLY accessing the internet on their phone.

That means their map of the territory is likely dramatically different from your map.

When people have different maps of the same territory miscommunication is inevitable. Miscommunication in business means you miss out on big opportunities.

To get a better understanding of how much your map is impacting the way you think, let's take a step back.

Take a careful look at the graph below. On it you'll find a line representing personal computer units shipped compared to smartphones and tablets shipped over a period spanning 1996 to 2017.

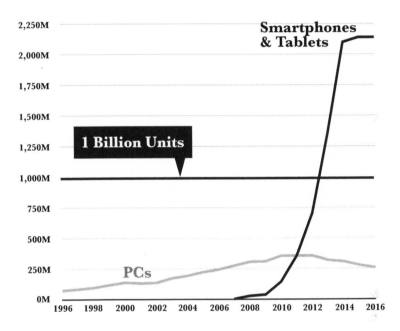

Now identify the first year you got on the internet. Then trace your finger along the line of PC units shipped up until the time when you got your first smartphone with internet access.

Realize that the only way that anyone got on the internet before the advent of the smartphone was with a personal computer. Remember, your potential of reaching people on the internet is directly proportional to their ability to access the internet.

So why did I start with Facebook's Mobile Moment?

If you connect the chart with PC vs. smartphone and tablets units shipped with Facebook's Mobile Moment, then you'll see that Facebook's Mobile Moment was created by the rocketing number of smartphones and tablets hitting the market, bringing over a billion additional people online.

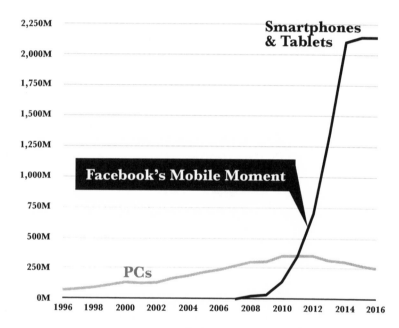

Seeing that Facebook, one of the most popular internet destinations, has a large majority of its traffic on mobile, you can imagine how that trend is impacting your business.

For me it wasn't until 2006 that I finally was able to get a business to be very profitable and successful by most anyone's description. Our success was based entirely on the growing trend of personal computers connected to the internet.

If a potential customer didn't have an email address and some way to access the internet, they never would have found out about our live trainings or been able to register and get the instructions on how to attend.

Further, they wouldn't have had the opportunity to learn how we could help them and then invest in our training and receive our guidance that would ultimately turn around their failing businesses.

Our success was directly connected to the number of prospective customers that had access to the internet. Maybe you've had a similar experience.

If we were able to have so much success in 2006, before the smartphone really took off, what would our success have looked like if that business started today?

This mobile shift has had a huge impact on your potential for success as well. In this book you will learn how to adjust your map so that you can clearly see the opportunity that this shift in the territory has presented.

You'll learn how the skewed map you've been using that comes from how **YOU** work is killing opportunities that are right in front of your nose.

You'll also become acutely aware of how natural the strategies and concepts you learn in this book will come to you, as well as how quickly you'll be able to adopt them. This will be due to the fact that they spring out of how you *already* communicate with your friends and family, coupled with your updated map

Once you finish this book you will probably be tempted to face-palm yourself because of how obvious these concepts are, but don't beat yourself up.

The world is always shifting around us and it's so easy to get comfortable with our out of date map... especially when the section of the map we've been using has delivered us to our desired destination in a speed and ease we've grown accustomed to.

The quickest way to change your results is to update your map. Just imagine how much more useful that Honda Pilot navigation system would be if I upgraded the map.

Get excited, because if you already have a successful business with your current map, and you update your map and employ the natural techniques you'll learn in this book, your revenue and profit are going to shift dramatically higher.

Before I go any further I need to share something very personal with you so that you understand **WHY** I wrote this book for *YOU*.

I can distinctly remember waking up one morning in early 2006 at 3am in a cold sweat.

"How in the world am I going to be able to support my family? I've got a wife and 5 kids who are depending on me and I have no clue what I'm doing!"

Have you been there?

My map of the territory was severely out of date. I had many pieces with great detail, but the part that had the X marking the treasure was missing.

If I hadn't met a friend that updated my map to include direct response marketing[1] and marketing automation[2], I would have continued to be in a very scary place of uncertainty and fear. I wouldn't have been able to progress in my journey with the confidence I now enjoy.

Fortunately, God led me to a guide that would help me fill in the blanks in the way I needed at that time and everything changed for me.

---

1 Direct Response Marketing is marketing that is designed to get the consumer of it to identify themselves with contact information. This is different than just getting someone aware of your business or offer in that it requires that an exchange of information occur. A direct response marketer is always thinking of how they can get a lead to identify themselves as part of the marketing process. If they spend money and don't end up with some contact information from interested parties, they consider the campaign to be a failure.

2 Marketing Automation is the usage of software, normally sold as a service with a monthly fee, to collect and organize contact information and automate communication with those contacts. There is a large variety of marketing automation platforms and they all have their strengths and weaknesses. I'd rather a business was using some marketing automation software than none. That being said, depending on the use case there are better solutions. I don't go into that in this book, but if you need guidance or are wondering if you have the right software for your solution, call or text my team at (949) 835-5300 and we'll be happy to point you in the right direction or confirm suspicions.

That's why I've written this book for you.

To serve as a guide to help you leave behind confusion, uncertainty, and maybe even fear about how to get the attention and contact information of prospective customers in a mobile era. To fill in the gaps on your map.

Chapter 1

THE EMAIL DILEMMA

In August of 2007 my brother Trent came to me and said, *"I've got an idea for a business that I know is going to be very important, and I want your help to build it."*

Maybe Trent's confidence in me was misplaced. Maybe it was because I was his oldest brother. Either way, we were in for a wild ride.

He was prophetic in his proclamation that what he had come up with would be really important.

If you recall, in late 2007 the mortgage melt down was beginning to really crash, and Trent had found a bank loss mitigator who was willing to explain to him how real estate agents needed to present their short sales in order to get them approved by the bank.

See, if you owed more to the bank than your house was worth and you wanted to sell it, you needed the bank's approval. And banks are ruthless. They were destroying homeowners and real estate agents alike in their desire to limit losses as home values tumbled.

When Trent called me, he had already set up our first sales presentation. He had a company send out an email about a seminar where a bank insider was going to reveal exactly what the bank was doing to real estate agent's commissions that was killing their business.

When Trent called he said there were twenty one agents scheduled to come, and he needed me to help finalize the offer.

Eleven of the twenty one agents in the room bought in spite of, or maybe because of, our over-the-top bank insider getting very raw with them about how banks worked and what he thought of real estate agents.

We were on to something.

But in 2007, Facebook was pretty much limited to a few college campuses, and Google Ad Words was super intimidating for a noob[3].

So we turned to paid emails sent through providers in the real estate markets across the United States to get the word out about our seminars.

---

3 I had just begun my marketing education in June of 2006 after moving back to Southern California. I was VERY wet behind the ears.

It ended up being so successful we did $1.3 million in sales during the first twelve months of operation.

Over the course of the next few years we would send out millions of emails to promote events and sell to our customers and prospects.

While we did include other methods of communication, like fax and voice broadcast[4] (*with hesitation*), we primarily emailed.

Because of my direct response marketing education I knew I needed to branch out, but email seemed like the only and best option.

Yet we were constantly fighting to get emails delivered. Every week we were learning new ways that email service providers worked to protect their customers from unwanted email.

In the years that followed we would end up getting to nearly $3 million in annual revenue all on the back of email.

But why so much dependence on email?

---

4 I've always hated the idea of communicating with others in a way that I find personally annoying, and I've always found voice broadcasts to be annoying. So even though I have the capability to do some pretty unique things with voice broadcast given my expertise, because I really hate it, I won't do it. When I did voice broadcasts at the time, I had a message that basically seemed like we had a bad connection and hung up if they answered, and then my real message was only delivered if voice mail picked up. Unfortunately for my team, if you call a real estate agent and have a bad connection, they will call you back, so when we did a broadcast to 1,000 agents, our phone lines would be inundated with call backs, wearing our team's nerves and leaving them frazzled. Needless to say, we couldn't do that too often and keep them around.

Most marketing software and CRMs[5] were built with email in mind. It's safe to say most are email centric.

This is not a big surprise because it's a natural progression of the PC Internet Paradigm. I mean, email is practically synonymous with PC Internet. And since most marketing software platforms are just iterations off whomever was the leader at the time, and because email is, on some levels, easy to implement, it has become the center of contact communication.

Personally, I believe if the Internet had been born on smartphones, instead of computer terminals, email would have never existed. We love it that much. ;)

The real allure of email comes because marketing software makes sending emails easy, not because it's the most effective means of communicating. In fact, in many softwares, sending an email is the **only** way to communicate with a contact.

Because this is the case, many folks are led to only think in terms of email when they think about communicating with their customer from a CRM or marketing software.

---

5 CRM is short for Client Relationship Management. Years ago ACT was one of the top CRM softwares available to small businesses, but many businesses use spreadsheets or quickbooks as their CRM. It's essentially a list of all your customers and prospects and the value of one depends largely on it's features. Marketing automation software is frequently used as a CRM although it may not be a true CRM. The truth is, they are usually sufficient, but may create issues at some point if they don't have true CRM capabilities. Not a big deal, but something to be aware of if you're at the phase of picking a software.

Add to that the fact that emails are very easy to collect, and you can see the basis for the *Email Dilemma*.

Maybe emails are so easy to collect because, from the contact's perspective, they're not very valuable. Maybe folks have just become accustomed to dealing with emails from businesses.

Either way, between the ease of using email and marketing software and the relative ease of collecting email addresses from contacts, people have become overly reliant on email as the principle or **only** way for communicating with contacts.

But is that really so bad?

Let's look at some of the hard facts about email. It's fairly common to be able to get between a 5% and, on the high side, 25% click-thru rate on an email.

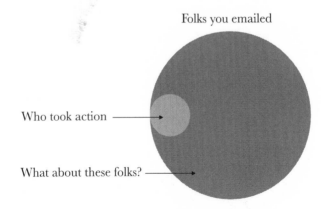

Folks you emailed

Who took action

What about these folks?

What does that actually mean?

It means that 75%-95% of the people you are emailing aren't taking any action.

"But Ryan, at least they are seeing my emails, right?"

Are they?

Some people like to talk about open rates, but open rates are virtually worthless. Open rates are based on the ability for a software to be able to track the opening of an image in the email body.

Many email service providers open images in advance of their user seeing the email to speed up the user experience, especially with the proliferation of smartphones, rendering the open rate virtually useless.

The open rate does not equal an actual view by a human, simply the opening of an image by a computer.

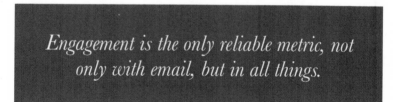

Engagement is the only reliable metric, not only with email, but in all things.

Taking all of this into consideration, you realize that 50-75% of all email subject lines, not even email bodies, aren't seen, much less evaluated.

This can be a pretty depressing picture if you're relying upon email alone. And to make it even worse, many folks are spending countless hours trying to make their emails more effective, writing and rewriting what we easily estimate will probably never be seen by more than half the people they are emailing.

Evolving Hurdles for Email Deliverability

In the early 2000s, the big challenge for email marketing was getting past spam filters, but it's become even tougher to give your email a fighting chance.

Now email service providers are using machine learning to filter out business messages and put them into different categories or folders, making it very easy for consumers to eliminate marketing emails without even seeing the email, the subject line, or who it's from.

When I first got started with marketing automation, I sent millions of emails to promote our business and get new customers. But as competitive as email marketing was then, it's a 1,000 times worse today.

Since then, millions of small businesses have discovered email marketing and are likewise sending trillions more emails than what was sent when I started in 2006.

The amount of competition in the email inbox can be daunting to think about. How can you get your prospect to engage with your company using email?

And if all of that wasn't bad enough, most people look at email as a chore, not something they enjoy doing.

Rather, it's something they have to filter through and clean out or avoid entirely. It's not uncommon to see phones with 5,000, 6,000, or 10,000 unread emails.

That tells you quite a bit about the story of working with emails alone.

But if the reality of email is really that bad, why do business owners continue to rely solely upon email?

I think it's because email is perceived to be free. Obviously it's not. The cost is baked into the cost of these marketing softwares or CRMs. In fact, even if email was free, even if it cost you nothing to send it, there is still a cost. A very expensive cost that almost nobody thinks about...

The Economics of Attention Currency

I call this cost attention cost.

Every communication that we attempt to make with a prospect or customer has a cost: their attention.

It costs them time and mental power to evaluate and look at our communications.

The economics of attention currency are that each time we communicate, we either make a deposit or withdrawal in the attention currency we carry with that contact.

If you send messages that don't create value from their perspective, then you have made a withdrawal from your attention currency account with that contact.

The more withdrawals you make, the more likely they are to ignore your messages entirely. Even if they go through the process of looking at their emails, they'll just delete your message before they open it if you've made too many withdrawals and not enough deposits.

This doesn't just apply to email. It holds true for all forms of communication with a contact.

Remember that.

Keep it in mind as you're creating campaigns or deciding on how you're going to communicate with a contact.

Ask yourself:

What is going to be the attention cost of this message?

Am I confident I'm making a deposit in my attention currency account with the contacts that will receive this?

You build a relationship with somebody by making deposits in the relationship. This happens when you deliver real value from **their** perspective.

I like to say if you can earn the heart, then you'll earn the money. In other words, all communication is about connection.

The beautiful thing about the tools you have available to you today is marketing automation software makes it possible to tailor your messages to the needs of your contacts.

The more tailored the message, the more perceived value it will carry to the contact.

Remember this concept as we go through the remainder of this book because it will serve you *richly*.

I know I've painted a pretty bleak picture for email, but email isn't all bad. It has a hidden upside.

40-60% of the emails that you have in your database will match to a custom audience on Facebook. That may be the biggest upside to collecting email addresses.

The fact that you have an email address means you might be able to identify that person on a social network, like Facebook or Instagram, and, as a result, target them with messages in the place where they actually enjoy spending time, which we all know, is **not** the email inbox.

I want you to break free from email dependence.

Not email *usage*, but email *dependence*.

The final piece that may keep you trapped in an addiction to email is your profit margin. I've noticed that the lower the profit margin, the more difficult it can be to wean the business off of email dependance.

It's outside of the scope of this book to fix your margins entirely. The easiest way to do that is to modify your business model to allow customers to buy from you more frequently, in larger orders, or both.

That being said, you'll find that as you apply what you learn in this book, doors of opportunity to increase your margin and adjust your business model will open naturally. For now you may just need to take my word for it, but by the time you finish this book, I have no doubt those opportunities will be crystal clear.

A First Step in the Right Direction

The first step you can take, even before you continue on to the next chapter, is to look at your existing email campaigns, if you have them, and ask, "*What other methods of communication could I employ to be able to deliver my message to my prospect that has a smartphone?*"

Don't decide what's possible based on what you know is possible, just ask the question, "*If I could communicate with my contact in any format, which format would give me the best results to be able to get that message in front of them in a way that would be good for them and would allow me to create more value for that contact?"*

As you start to think in this way and put down on paper ideas of what you might include to enhance or supplement your email-only campaigns, you're starting down the right path to reap massive rewards.

Sales come from conversations.

People buy because they get enough information and enough trust in a company that they feel they can spend money with them and get the outcome that they're looking for. This trust can be built through conversations.

Remember: Nobody wants your emails.

In fact, nobody wants any communication from you.

What they really want is to have their problem solved or their dream achieved. They will only willingly and excitedly accept your messages, in whatever method of communication you choose, when they perceive that it will help them along their journey to getting what they want.

Zig Ziglar might have said it best, *"You can get everything in life you want, if you will just help other people get what they want."*

Recommended Methods of Communication

Personally, I like text messages, direct voicemails, Facebook ads, and direct mail as supplemental avenues for delivering my message...in addition to email.

If you've watched my videos online or listened to my podcast, you may get the impression that I absolutely hate email and don't even use it.

The reality is, email does have a place in this world.

We've grown accustomed to it. People have email addresses. Let's not neglect it, but at the same time, let's not rely so heavily upon it that it becomes an albatross around our neck.

Chapter 2

HOW YOU SEE
CONTACTS

As a kid, every Saturday morning I'd wake up and watch cartoons, at least until my old man would call us out to wash cars in the driveway.

Loony Tunes had a character called Chicken Hawk that was always after Foghorn Leghorn. Chicken Hawk frequently saw Foghorn as a cooked chicken, complete with those little white things covering the chicken leg bones.

In essence, Chicken Hawk saw Foghorn as food instead of the dynamic character he really was. How Chicken Hawk saw Foghorn defined their relationship.

---

*How do you see the contacts that are
in your marketing software?*

How you see your contacts defines your relationship and changes how you communicate with them.

Have you ever heard the phrase, *"the money is in the list"*? If you have, what do you think of that phrase?

Let me give you another phrase to think about: *"The money is in the relationship with the people on my list."* Which of those two phrases rings more true to you?

If *the money is in the list* rings true to you, it implies that you see people as moneybags, sort of like Chicken Hawk sees Foghorn as a cooked chicken.

Don't look at people as money bags. It's bad.

When you see people as moneybags instead of as people just like you, it changes the way you'll communicate with them in a bad way.

Socially, you should know, and probably are almost compelled to feel, that the proper answer is that you see that **money *is in the relationship with the people*** on your list. But what you do speaks louder than what you think or even say.

Let's look at how you communicate with people in your marketing software.

Do you speak **at** people?

Look at your emails and see if they are just telling people to *do* things or if they lead to a *conversation* with them.

Frequently, when I read emails sent by marketing automation software, they are speaking *at* me, not *with* with me.

In fact, many people would even prefer that the contacts never respond. They don't even want to hear from them. They just want prospects to buy their product or service and get out of their life.

That's not to say that there are not times when you will need to lead folks with a direct call to action in any communication. That can be very powerful. But what you're looking for is an emphasis of speaking *with* people.

Another situation that causes people to see contacts as moneybags instead of as people is slim margins.

Slim margins mean I can't justify spending time with people. As a result, I will build barriers to prevent people from taking my time. That reasoning is perfectly understandable, but that doesn't mean it's right.

This is why I said in the previous chapter that you have to make sure you have sufficient margins to be able to invest your[6] time with the people who need it.

The reality is, not everybody that will buy from you will need your time or want to communicate with you. But for those that do, **making yourself available** will dramatically increase your profits, assuming you can maintain an acceptable profit margin in your business.

What I hope you do is you see contacts as people. When you see contacts as people, you're going to invite them to take action because you want them to get the thing they're looking for. You'll be starting conversations and you'll be glad you did.

All the Money is in the Long Term View

Higher margins will allow you to welcome interactions in your business. But admittedly, when you haven't

---

6 Please note that when I say your time, I mean either you personally or your team. Honestly I don't get to spend as much personal time with our clients and customers as I used to. My role has shifted as our businesses have grown. But because I make a point of picking good people, I'm able to maintain good quality and transparency in the personal communication that goes on with my customers.

been engaging in those conversations, it can feel impossible to get started.

I've often heard business owners raise the concern that if they let their customers call or text them, the cost will put them out of business. I certainly understand why they might feel that way.

If you've been primarily using email for all your prospect and customer interaction, you know how time consuming that can be. What you haven't considered is that using email for sales and support is hell on earth.

The transfer of information is so slow compared to text chat or phone call. Couple that with the fact that you have to enter into the jaws of hell itself, *the email inbox*, to get that information, and you'd be kinder to your contacts to water board them.

What we discovered when we moved from email only to personal engagement via text and phone calls is that the time it took to answer sales questions and customer support needs was a fraction of what it was when we were relying on email.

See, when you engage with contacts, prospects, and customers in direct personal communication, inevitably your margins go up because you are now creating relationships instead of just transactions.

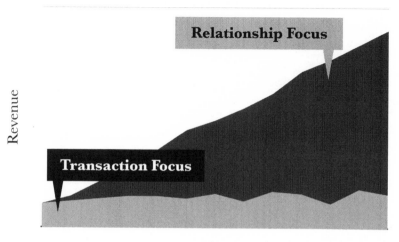

Revenue

Relationship Focus

Transaction Focus

Time

All the money in business is in long-term relationships, even if the person isn't going to spend money long term with you.

For example, a house purchase is probably not something that's going to happen every month or year. Studies show that the average person will buy a home every seven years. That is not a relationship where you'll see money on a regular basis from the relationship.

But a long term relationship with a customer that bought a home generates referrals, and referrals generate money.

Investing in relationships, even if your customers can't buy from you frequently, is always worthwhile. Besides all that, it's much more enjoyable to work with people.

If you don't want to work with the people that currently buy your services or product, then **stop**.

Change your business.

Start working with people you enjoy. Life is too short for you to work with people you don't like.

I personally love working with business owners. I get how they think. We see the world very similarly. Because of that, I really enjoy working with them. I love helping them get massive results. And, even more importantly, I know what's at stake for them.

That doesn't mean I like working with all business owners though. Business owners that really get under my skin are the blamers and the complainers. They're like nails on a chalkboard to me. Fortunately, they are few and far between and they really don't last very long as entrepreneurs.

Make sure that you love the people you're working with because starting and having conversations is the basis for real growth in a company.

I personally **love** to help companies see exciting growth from two common scenarios:

1. A company is doing well, relying principally on marketing to produce orders with a heavy reliance on email marketing. We help them introduce text

message conversations to non-converting leads in a number of simple ways, and then sales go through the roof. In fact, doubling sales isn't too uncommon.

2. A company is doing well with marketing and sales, but they are selling old school by just pounding the phones. We help them introduce conversations and other medias into the sales process and dramatically increase the number of conversations they are having per hour of effort. And again, doubling sales isn't unusual.

This is why a love for the people you'll have as customers is so critical. Engaging in conversations can have such a positive impact, but I feel it's best if that doesn't suck the life out of you in the process!

Mobile is Inherently Intimate

When it comes to mobile communication, it's important to realize that it is inherently very intimate.

The smartphone is rarely more than three feet away from the owner. As a result, any communication that comes through it is intimate by definition.

So if you care about the folks you're communicating with and you're going to take a mobile focus, then you really want to be aware of the order of intimacy[7] of each channel as you decide to incorporate it into your campaigns and strategy.

Because smartphones natively support email, phone call, voicemails, text messaging, and social networking, make sure that you're really delivering what they perceive to be valuable in each communication. You'll want to think about how you incorporate those medias into your communication strategy.

Our phones are such a big part of our lives now that, according to Statista.com[8], most people spend 3+ hours a day on the smartphone versus just 2 hours a day on computers or PCs.

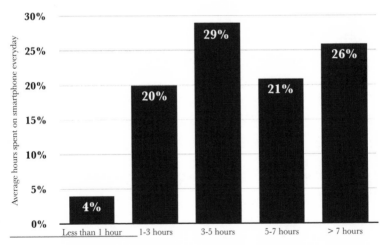

7 Each channel you use to communicate with contacts has an intimacy level. Email, for example, is very commercial, but also used for personal communication. So it's not completely cold, but it certainly would be perceived as less intimate. A text message is dominantly one on one communication, so its intimacy level is high. A social media ad is mixed in with personal posts from friends, so it's more intimate than an email, but less than a text message. You want to consider each channel you have available to you and order them according to intimacy level and tailor your message accordingly. The power of each message will be enhanced as it matches with its intimacy level.

8 https://www.statista.com/statistics/781692/worldwide-daily-time-spent-on-smartphone/

To build relationships on mobile, tune the messaging to match the intimate nature of the context.

You may have noticed that I've been talking about marketing automation software as if it were a given. This is because I consider it to be a given.

You must use some marketing automation software or customer relationship management system. It's just a requirement now[9].

On that note, one of the things that I've seen when it comes to how we communicate with people, especially when we first get introduced to this exciting new technology of automation, is a tendency to over-automate.

This, in and of itself, is an indication of seeing people as moneybags instead of people.

Have you ever been in an automated chatbot loop or gone through a phone tree from hell?

Or, maybe you've received email after email after email and you realize, *these are coming from a machine. This person isn't really writing to me.* It was obvious right from the start because of the tone and nature of the communication.

---

9 The nature of technology is that as it advances, you must keep in pace with it or be left behind. The truth about marketing automation software is it makes a small business able to compete against much larger businesses with large budgets and armies of workers. When used properly by a small business it can make that small business much more powerful than a larger organization because it can nearly eliminate the inconsistencies of human nature from the organization without stripping your company of its humanity. Humanity IS the most valuable currency of this century. Mark my words…

If you have, then you've experienced over automation.

Over automation does not build relationships.

Bots do have a purpose. I'm not a huge fan of them, but they can be used for answering very basic questions.

The reason why that connection is so important is people don't do business with nameless, faceless corporations willingly. But, they love to do business with other people because people are naturally social creatures.

> *Technology is only good if it mitigates the impact of human nature without reducing your humanity, that connection between two people that is so critical in creating a relationship[10].*

Don't over automate things, especially in communication with contacts. The best way to discover what you should automate is to look at where your human nature would break down.

---

10 I want to clarify. When I say creating a relationship, I don't mean to going out to dinner with your contacts and spending personal time with them. What I do mean is that you're connecting with them as one human connects with another.

Where would you forget to communicate?

What would you not do reliably?

As humans, one of our failings is we tend to forget the important things that we need to do. We aren't very reliable at communicating in the way we know we should. We want to use marketing automation to lessen the impact of our forgetful natures.

Create marketing automation campaigns with the perspective that you are communicating with another human being *(another living, breathing person who has needs, wants, desires, dreams, hopes, and aspirations)*. Then, as you craft your communication and choose which ways you'll communicate with them, you'll be more personal and create a better connection with them.

> *Use how you would interact with people naturally in the sales process to guide your automation plan.*

In this way, we are enhancing our humanity or our capacity to connect with another human being.

Make sure that people can respond and engage in a conversation with you so they can get the information they need to make the best buying decision for themselves.

As you see people as agents to themselves, capable of and needing to make decisions based on their own self interests, you'll discover that life gets much better. You will enjoy selling. You will enjoy teaching, prospecting, and getting people to learn about your business and become customers.

Your team members will be happier because they'll have more open and sincere communication with the people that you serve. And, as a result, they'll feel better about the work that they're doing.

Remember, **see people for who they truly are**- human beings going through the same experience that you and I are going through.

We are all trying to do our best to get what we want and what we hope for out of this life. This view will make it easier for you to connect with them and help them to achieve their dreams, solve problems, or alleviate pain that is in their life.

With that, we're ready for what I consider to be the most important rule of marketing ever discovered: **Marketing Rule #19**.

Chapter 3

MARKETING RULE #19

When I was attending college, I had to take organic chemistry because I was intending to become a dentist. Fortunately, I did not. If you've seen my hands, you would know these mitts are huge and probably wouldn't be very comfortable in someone's mouth.

My professor for this class was also a chemist at Baskin Robbins 31 Flavors. As we were chatting one day during lab, he explained that flavoring science isn't taught in schools. In fact, it's only taught inside of corporations and is heavily guarded and protected because of all the money that can be made from flavoring.

As a result, he couldn't even teach us the flavoring chemistry because he was bound by contracts.

In a similar fashion, this seems as though it's also true in the marketing world; marketing that actually works is hard to come by in the educational system. I've talked to many people who have advanced degrees in marketing who said they didn't really learn anything useful until they got out of college.

The reality is, most small businesses getting into marketing automation software don't know the basics of marketing. And, you really can't blame them. Really understanding marketing and how to use it in a way that will actually produce results for a small business takes a good bit of effort.

Marketing for small businesses is different than and has to be much more effective than marketing for large corporations with huge budgets and teams of people. Because of that, the best marketing techniques are discovered in small businesses that master them.

When you're working with marketing automation software, which is designed to make marketing better and easier, and you don't understand marketing, you can run into some really big challenges.

One of those challenges is marketing myths that are propagated by gurus, books and seminars. Frankly, there is no one standing as the guardian of truth for what is really working in marketing for small business.

There is also intense social pressure on gurus to always share something new and exciting. This need to impress that also destroys our news networks can lead to fake marketing news being presented as well vetted and proven strategies.

This effect of needing to present new and innovative ideas can lead to the establishment of *"sacred cows"*: rules that everybody follows without question.

One of those is that the less contact information you ask for, the better the conversion.

Is that true?

Yes, you will get more leads when you ask for less contact information, and it kind of stands to reason, doesn't it?

If I'm asking for contact information from you and I only ask for the email address, you probably have several email addresses you can give me.

In fact, you have one that's reserved just for junk mail, don't you? You would gladly give that to me, especially if you don't know or trust me yet. And, as a result, it stands to reason that the less contact information you asked for, the more conversions you'll get.

The more important question is: Is it useful for making money to ask for less contact information? The answer is a resounding **no**.

In that business my brother and I started that went from $0 to $1.3 million in 12 months, the registration form that we used to get people to attend our sales pitch asked for their name, email address, office number, mobile phone number, fax number, physical address, and boss' name.

Interestingly, we had people give us **all** of that information on a regular basis. But at one point, a few years in, we started to have a little bit of a decline in registrations for our trainings.

I thought, *"Well, people say the less information you ask for the more conversions you'll have, so why not ask for less information and see if we can get a boost in our registrations for our events?"*

We cut down our form dramatically, asked for much less information, and guess what happened?

Registrations still went down[11].

The **real** solution was to *increase the perceived value of what we were offering* to the marketplace. We did that, returned to our previous registration form, asking for everything and the dog, and registrations went back up.

So **Marketing Rule #19** came from our own experience in our own business and our experience helping thousands of small business owners dramatically increase their profits.

---

11 Thank goodness too. Because if registrations had gone up, I might have fallen for one of the biggest scams perpetuated on the small business world since the advent of the internet. I would have believed that asking for less information was the answer and missed learning the most important truth you can learn: that lead capture conversion has more to do with the perceived value of the offering from the lead's perspective than how much information you ask for. And we would have been at a disadvantage relative to Marketing Rule #19.

Because I was asking for name, phone number, mobile phone number, fax, boss' name, and address, I knew with nearly 99% confidence that I could reach that contact. I could communicate with them in some form or another.

Compare that to somebody relying on email alone trying to reach the same audience.

Who do you think would do more business? Me, with the name and the phone number and the email address, the fax number, the physical address, and the mobile phone number? Or the guy that just has an email address? Sure, he has a lot more email addresses than I do, but what could he do to communicate with those contacts compared to what I could do?

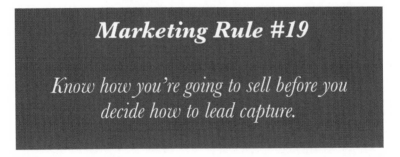

Marketing Rule #19

Know how you're going to sell before you decide how to lead capture.

When you capture a lead, you have determined how you can sell.

If you capture a lead that is a name and email address, you can only sell by email. If you capture a mobile phone number, a name, and a email address, now you have a whole host of options.

You can email them.

You can call them.

You can text them, if you get their permission.

You can re-market to them on Facebook.

Of all these ways of communicating, my favorite is the mobile phone number.

Scan for a special video

*The average person only has
one mobile phone number.*

Why? Because it costs money to get a real mobile phone number.

The average person has two or more email addresses.

I have a friend who's about 65 years old. He's an old cowboy. He's got a smartphone with a junk email address that receives 300+ emails a day and a personal email address he doesn't give out to anybody except for his friends, which he actually checks. Oh, and he has *one* mobile phone number.

As you are strategically deciding what information you need to gather in the lead generation process so that you can sell effectively, remember to focus on communication channels where people are more likely to spend time.

As I said before, email is a chore.

It's extremely competitive.

You have to deal with fake email addresses. It's extremely difficult to know a junk email address from the email address that they actually check.

You also have the issue of dealing with spam trap emails that are put out there to reduce your ability to deliver emails to those who actually want them.

If all that isn't enough, it's not even somewhere people enjoy spending their time.

One place where people don't mind spending their time is text messaging.

They already use it in conversations with their friends and relatives. It's short. It's to the point.

It's easy to be personable and conversational versus promotional in text messages.

And, like we all know, your contacts have their phone next to them and they see their text messages. Push notifications are always on for text messages.

It is a great media if you use it properly, which you're already learning how to do in this book.

The final place where people enjoy spending time is on social networks. In fact, people can't keep themselves off of social networks. My wife has deleted Facebook several times, *which also implies she's installed it several times.*

People really can't keep themselves off of social networks. Part of this goes back to what I said before; we are inherently social creatures. We want to interact, we want to see what's going on with other people. Because of that, you know social media is a place where people are going to spend their time. You need to learn how to master that as part of your marketing process.

Social networks especially require an understanding of interruption-based marketing, which hinges on keeping people in the mobile experience.

If you're doing anything with Facebook or Instagram, for example, you have to make sure that the experience stays mobile[12] and isn't dependent on a desktop experience, which is the mistake that many make.

---

12 Oli Billson and I recorded a great episode for my podcast on this topic. It's about an hour and 45 minutes long. Text **PODCAST** to **(949) 835-5300** to get a link to it.

Marketing Rule #19 and Facebook Lead Ads

Facebook ads created quite a stir when they first came on the scene, but excitement has died off because many people didn't know and still don't know how to use them.

Some of the biggest names in Facebook marketing don't use Facebook lead ads because they don't understand the concepts that you've already been exposed to so far in this book.

Lead ads are essentially web forms Facebook has built into its native apps that open up when a person clicks on an ad. What's really exciting about lead ads is they come pre-filled. They already have the name of the contact, their phone number, their email address, and whatever other information you asked for that is already stored in the Facebook Network.

This means that your contacts won't have to type in any of their contact information with those french-fry-eating fingers. This is a huge relief for me, Mr. Lincoln Log fingers. The prospect also doesn't have to make a decision about which email address to give you because it's already right there.

I get really excited about Facebook lead ads because of another company that my brother Trent and I started. In this company, we generated over 70,000 leads over the course of two years at the cost of $1.65 per lead.

As we did an evaluation on these leads, we discovered that 97% of the phone numbers we asked for were mobile phone numbers. 99.6% were real phone numbers. 76% of these leads also explicitly gave us permission to text them right off the bat.

Because of that, we could help people make a buying decision using text, call, retargeting on Facebook and Instagram, and finally, email.

If we didn't know about Marketing Rule #19, we wouldn't have thought to ask for the name, email, mobile phone number, and permission to text them. We would have only had email to sell with and the business would have become untenable.

It would have been impossible to have the margins the business has because of the limitation of being bound to only market, communicate, and sell through email.

I hope you'll memorize Marketing Rule #19, which is: *Before you decide how to lead capture, know how you're going to sell.*

When you do that, you'll make smart decisions in your lead capture process. And, with the rest of the things you learn in this book, you're going to be dramatically shifting your business to higher profits, higher margins, and increased excitement about working with people.

Chapter 4

OLD SKOOL TEXTING

When I first got involved with text messaging for business, I started working with a company that provided short code text messages.

Short codes are those five to six digit numbers that people will frequently use in text message lead capture promotion at the corporate level.

Carriers originally created short codes to isolate and profit from promotional text messages that big corporations were wanting to send out.

See, every single phone on the market today, whether it be "dumb phone" or smartphone, all have one app installed on them the day they are activated: the text messaging app. Texting has always been a big deal.

Carriers identified an opportunity to charge an additional delivery fee per message sent for business text messages, in particular, promotional text messages. These are the kind of text messages a company might send to get people to quickly go to their store and buy.

For example:

> Today we have a sale for 15% off at all Nordstrom Rack locations in San Diego. Just show this message to receive your discount!
> We'll see you soon!

That promotional type message is exactly what short codes were created to deliver.

The big strength of the short code is this ability to get priority delivery of text messages through the networks. You can have 10,000 messages per minute sent out through a short code, something that's impossible for normal phone numbers[13].

However, that comes at a cost.

---

13 Normal phone numbers can only send one text message per second or 60/minute.

Short Code Weaknesses

While a short code does have the ability to handle high volumes of messages in short time periods, they also have many downsides that make them a poor fit for most businesses and most use cases.

A short code is expensive to operate.

It can cost anywhere from $1,000-$3,000 dollars per month to have access to a short code. Because of this, short code operators have some serious constraints on them that you don't have with the normal phone number.

Short codes are commonly shared among hundreds or thousands of companies. Because of this, knowing who a text is intended for gets complicated. In order to identify which of the hundreds of businesses an incoming text message is intended for, providers issue keywords.

A keyword is a single unique word that is associated with a business and usually has an automated text response or responses it will send to a person when they text the keyword to the short code.

Sounds like a good solution right?

But there are some issues inherent in this arrangement.

First, **you can't reliably carry on a one-on-one conversation** with a contact unless they were to start every conversation with the short code with the keyword assigned to your business.

Next, because **each keyword has to be unique**, *simple to text keywords are quickly picked by smart businesses,* which leaves you with hard to spell keywords that might even be changed by spellcheck. The plus side is you have to get really creative to get a good keyword with established short code providers.

Having a funky keyword is annoying and probably will lead to missing a few leads. But what's really devastating is the inability to have one-on-one conversations with contacts.

Not Normal

Additionally, **the five to six digits is not normal**. You commonly text to normal phone numbers, so that feels natural. Five to six digits throw people off.

I remember the first time I used a short code for lead capture. As I gave people the keyword that was assigned to me by the short code provider and the short code for them to text to, they were confused. I had them come up to me after I got off the stage and say, *"What number am I supposed to text to again? I got the keyword, but what else was I supposed to text you?"*

People didn't even know where to put the short code in on their phone. I'm sure it's gotten better since 2008, but it's still awkward for people and not as easy for them to grasp as a normal phone number.

Short Codes = Promotion

People have also now grown to understand that **a short code means promotion**. They're leery to get involved with a short code because they know they're going to get hit up with promotions on a regular basis as a result of interacting with that short code.

Finally, *you can't call from a short code*.

One of the big benefits of using normal phone numbers is the ability to have texting and calling occur on the same number, just like you do with your personal mobile phone.

This is natural. It's how people already communicate. It carries a lot of weight. As you read the next chapter that weight will be come self evident.

Perhaps the most negative characteristic of short codes is the **shared reputation**.

Unanticipated Shared Reputation

The shared reputation wasn't something that was intended by short code providers or the carriers, but it's a natural consequence of multiple businesses sharing the same number.

There once was an insurance company that saw the value of capturing mobile phone numbers through a text message lead generation process.

They signed up with a short code provider and created a million-dollar campaign that consisted of billboards, bus wraps, and signage all over the major cities. The campaign was actually working quite well.

Then, the short code provider signed up a adult entertainment company. I'm not sure if they knew they were signing up an adult entertainment company, but this adult entertainment company started sending out adult related text messages, which is not looked upon favorably by the carrier networks. As a result, the carrier shut down the short code.

It would have been bad enough to have that same phone number associated with this big insurance company and the adult entertainment company, but almost as bad, the million dollars that the insurance company had spent on signage and promotion of this big campaign was rendered useless overnight.

In order for this company to recover this campaign, they would have to get another third-party short code provider and swap out the phone number on all their advertising.

What a total nightmare.

While that's a very expensive mistake, what's most commonly going to occur for people that utilize short codes is that, inevitably, there will be an overlap of contacts between the multiple businesses using the short code.

Whether you like it or not, your reputation is now intertwined with another company's reputation.

Because of this, many large corporations have taken to owning their own short code[14]. They can't afford to have their reputation co-mingled with the reputation of another company not of their choice.

Strict Legal Requirements

Because of the special privileges that short codes have, they also have special requirements. **They have awkward legal wording** that's required in the first interaction somebody has with you via text message.

It's actually a good thing you can't carry on a one-on-one conversation with a short code. Since the initial text messages are so weird, I think it would just ruin the experience.

---

14 Political campaigns, like that of Donald Trump, get their own dedicated short code.

When it comes to texting, whether it's old school or new school, there are always legal concerns around texting. Laws and regulations are created to keep shady characters out or to give a competitive advantage to *well-connected* donors.

The big key to keeping yourself out of trouble is to open the door to texting early on in the relationship.

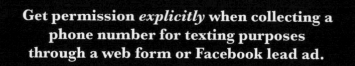

Get permission *explicitly* when collecting a phone number for texting purposes through a web form or Facebook lead ad.

Don't promote, *communicate* via text message.

Use something we call conversation starters to engage with the contact. I'll go into more detail on this in subsequent chapters.

And, of course, pay attention to attention currency.

When you engage people in conversation versus talking at them, when you deliver value and you don't pester, then texting becomes a powerful communication channel for you to be able to connect with and form relationships with prospects and customers.

Let's get into the exciting part where we delve deep into what you should be doing with text messaging to really connect with people on their phone.

Chapter 5

NEW SKOOL TEXTING

When I talk about new school texting, I'm talking about text messaging through a normal phone number, but with *special powers*.

Lead Capture: Automated Messaging Conversations

When it comes to lead capture, **keywords are the secret**.

Keywords are used for lead capture to identify the context of why someone is texting in to you and to allow you to gather some basic contact information before you segue into a live conversation.

Keywords for normal numbers are different from short codes for a number of reasons.

First, you're not competing with anyone else for these keywords, since you own your own number. Second, they are used for context, not identifying who gets the message. You always get all messages texted to your number.

What's really cool about keywords for lead capture is it's a simple lead capture mechanism that you can memorize. You'll have a virtual lead capture mechanism that can go anywhere.

When a contact texts your keyword to your phone number, it will initiate an automated messaging conversation.

This is usually consists of a couple steps of chat between a machine and your prospect that is designed to capture lead info so you can start a sales conversation or nurture through follow up.

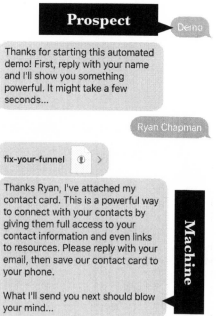

The beautiful thing about having your own phone number versus a shared short code when it comes to text message lead capture is the ability to choose whatever keyword you want.

A keyword should be a **simple, short, easy-to-spell** word. I like to type the word into my own phone and see if spellcheck tries to change the word. If it does, that's a good indication that I should choose another word.

Nobody really loved participating in spelling bees, except for the weirdos *(sorry if you're a weirdo)*, so don't make people have to spell long, complicated words. The added benefit of using a short, easy keyword is it makes it easier for you to memorize, too!

A few more guidelines include:

Avoid using people's names. When you are collecting contact information in an automated messaging conversation and you've used a name as a keyword, you can create a very undesirable loop for those folks!

Avoid using words that commonly are used to start a sentence. This isn't an issue for most texting services because they don't support live, one-on-one texting, but the system you'll want to use will[15], and using words commonly used to start a sentence can

---

15 If you would like my recommendation, text my team at (949) 835-5300 and we'll ask you a few questions to help determine which texting system would be best for you.

lead to folks who want to have a conversation with you going through an automated messaging conversation.

This is a lesson I learned the hard way. As me and my team were pioneering many of the lead capture methods used in text messaging, we got a little excited.

We used keywords like NOW, MOBILE and WOW. Granted, those selections were made before we discovered the importance of one-on-one texting as part of an overall mobile strategy. Yet as we began to focus more on conversation starters *(you'll learn more in this chapter, so keep reading)*, we discovered that folks were getting pulled into automated conversations because we were eliciting responses like "WOW!".

Avoid using texting opt out words like, STOP, UNSUBSCRIBE, QUIT, etc. Carriers have reserved these keywords for allowing folks to indicate that you shouldn't text them back.

Where Can You Use Text Message Lead Capture?

You can use a phone number and a keyword to capture leads virtually anywhere. You may have noticed, I've got a few of them in this book!

Direct mail is a great place to be using text message lead capture.

An text message call to action is by far better than a website URL. It requires about the same level of trust or confidence for someone to type in a website URL as it does for them to type in a keyword and a phone number, but there's a dramatic difference.

When somebody texts a keyword to your phone number, you already know why they're texting, and you now have their mobile phone number even if they didn't do anything else with you.

You've got that information, which means you could call them, you could text them a question, or you could re-market to them using Facebook custom audiences. And you know exactly why they texted in the first place, meaning you have context for all your follow-up communication.

It's tough to do that with a website visit.

Another great place to use a text message call to action is on a **business card**.

Text **DEMO** to
(760) 621-8199
to see how it works!

You can see here, I've got an example of asking people to text a keyword to a phone number in order for them to experience a demonstration of a product or service. This is a fantastic way to make your business card a lead capture device.

I love to add my text message call to action in **blog posts**.

This allows me to write about whatever topic that would be of interest to my prospective customers or existing customers and get them to raise their hand and show that they agree by giving them a text message call to action.

What's really great about the texting services I use is setting up a text message lead capture automated conversation takes just minutes. And connecting that conversation to a campaign in marketing automation software is simple.

I don't have to have any technical expertise. I don't need to know how to do CSS or HTML; I just pick a keyword following the guidelines in this book, create a conversation to collect the contact information I'll need to sell well *(Marketing Rule #19)*, and put the text message call to action in my blog post or direct mail piece or any of the myriad of other options available!

I wire up that conversation to my marketing automation software and in less than ten minutes I've got a new lead capture mechanism in place. You can eliminate all of the hurdles that normally slow down lead capture activities online or otherwise!

Social media posts also lend themselves very well to text message call to actions.

Just as with blog posts, when you make a social media post of any kind, include the keyword and phone number and a call to action. This approach pairs well with images, videos, live broadcasts, or just plain old text!

Possibly my favorite text message call to action is adding them to my **videos**. If you create a really good content focused video, one that people might even want to rip off and put on their own website, by overlaying a text message call to action, you have lead capture going wherever that video goes. That's powerful.

With the training business my brother and I started in 2007, we were creating industry leading content videos and it was very common for folks to embed our videos on their website and then use them to promote their own business. Adding a text message call to action to those videos would have allowed us to benefit from their *sharing*.

We both know that not everyone who watches a video is going to text in the keyword, but that's not really the point. A video acts as a sorter. When it's viewed by the right audience, they want to take the next step. By including a text message call to action, you give the right person the opportunity to take the next step and build future opportunities for yourself.

You deserve those opportunities, so *don't short change yourself.* Make a personal commitment to **always have a keyword and phone number on hand** when you record a video and always include a text message call to action.

While it is very simple to put together a new text message call to action and wire it up to your marketing automation platform, you don't need a bunch of unique keywords and campaigns for every single video.

In fact, I recommend having one primary keyword and number that you use repeatedly. However, as you progress as a marketer you may decide to use unique keywords that connect to the same campaign in order to allow you to identify the best videos or platforms to promote based on the number and quality of leads each produces, but that's a phase two action.

The classic use case for a keyword and phone number is **from the stage**.

Presenting from the stage has its own rules.

The biggest mistake is waiting to show your keyword and phone number until the last slide.

I've seen too many people make this classic mistake thinking that all they had to do was present the keyword and the phone number and people would just text in.

Show it early on in a presentation and keep the text message call to action, the keyword and phone number, at the top of all your slides after that.

As the audience's trust level in you goes up, they are more likely to text you. And, if you do it right, you can get **over 100% lead capture** from a room.

Sound impossible?

Let me tell you a story.

One of our clients, Story Brand, run by a very dynamic speaker, Don Miller, was presenting at a conference. He did a great presentation and because he had consulted with me ahead of time, he knew what to do.

He showed the call to action early and frequently throughout the remainder of his presentation. Because the presentation was good and because his call to action was so valuable to the members of the audience, not only did they all text in, they actually sent the keyword and the phone number to friends and business associates that they thought would benefit from what Don had to offer.

As a result, *Don ended up with nearly a **110%** of in the room texting in*. They captured a bonus 10-15% from folks sharing the keyword and phone number over their social networks and through text message.

Can you imagine what a difference capturing 110% of the rooms you speak to would make in your business?

When you deliver the text message call to action properly with the right offer in front of the right group, you can produce similar results.

Because of the mobility of the keyword/phone number lead capture mechanism, it makes it easy to share.

And just as you can use this lead capture mechanism in so many places, so can your fans as they share it with people they think would benefit from what you do.

You can also use a text message lead capture at a **networking event** or with somebody you meet the grocery store. It really can be used virtually anywhere because it's so easy to remember and because everyone you run into has a phone on them.

It's a really great way to start a conversation and to get people to raise their hand and identify themselves as people who are interested in learning more about the solutions that your business provides.

The Return of the Humble QR Code

With iOS 11, Apple made QR codes something that could be used again in the United States. While QR codes never lost popularity in Asian countries, in the West interest waned when Apple failed to bake in QR code reading into the phone. With the release of iOS 11, the native camera app on Apple devices automatically detects and converts QR codes into clickable buttons.

Now QR codes are a great way to add a simple and fun way for people to interact with your text message call to action on printed materials, in presentations, on slides, and on booth signs.

Flip a couple pages back and find the back of the business card example. Open your camera app and point it at the QR code on the page. Tap the button, then tap the button to open your messaging app. Notice the keyword and phone number are pre-filled, just waiting for you to hit send!

When it comes to QR Codes I want you to check out https://www.qrcode-monkey.com/. It's totally free as of the time I'm writing this book and I think it's awesome for creating some really cool QR Codes that are great for direct mail, the web, and slides.

Text message lead capture is really great for collecting mobile phone numbers, as that happens automatically, in addition to email addresses, names, and very short answers.

Because entering in data on a smartphone isn't a fun process, I avoid asking people to text back long answers as part of a text message lead capture process.

Because of advances in machine learning on smartphones, when you ask the question just right, the phone may even recommend the answer to the contact, making it even easier to answer questions like, *"what is your name?"* and, *"what is your email address?"*

One thing we've discovered that text message lead capture is not good for is collecting mailing addresses.

It's just too easy for that address to get broken up or sent over in the wrong way, so your data integrity goes down. At that point you now have to get a human involved, which defeats the whole purpose of an automated conversation. Avoid trying to collect addresses directly through a text message conversation.

Open The Door To Texting

Text message conversations are great for opening the door to texting.

Because the first text is being sent by the contact to you, they're being introduced to the concept that your business does text messaging.

This is really good news for a number of reasons, but one of them is that, according to Pew Research Center[16], adults prefer texting over phone calls and emails.

It's interesting to note that, during that week long study, 97% of the participants used text messaging vs 88% using email.

100% of the 18-29 year olds texted, which isn't really a surprise to anyone.

But 98% of the participants aged 30-49 years old texted. That's good news because for many businesses, this is their prime age demographic.

92% of those 50+ years old texted during the week. So texting isn't just for young people. The 50+ age demographic also holds most of the disposable income in the world.

---

16 http://www.pewinternet.org/2015/04/01/us-smartphone-use-in-2015/

Just remember, *everyone is doing it,* and *every device sold supports it.*

It's useful to note that phone calls ranked in next at 93%. In other words, folks use their phones for texting, then calling, and then email. Fascinating, isn't it?

Automated Messaging Conversation Guidelines

When you are creating an automated text message conversation, there are a few important things to consider.

First, **have a couple of steps in your text message conversation**.

While it is possible to have them text in the keyword and immediately get whatever they're looking for sent to them in the first text, that doesn't quite open the door for texting the same way that a multi-step conversation does.

I recommend at least 2-3 steps.

I frequently will **ask for name and then email**. That order is important too.

Asking for the name first and email second allows you to collect the information that you need to have the most options to be able to sell later ... Marketing Rule #19!

In your **first response**, make sure that it's a **plain old SMS**[17], meaning text only and under 160 characters.

Text only messages are routed through a faster pathway on the carrier networks, making the response

---

17 SMS stands for Simple Messaging Service and is text only, limited to 160 characters. Emojis are equal to 2-3 characters.

almost instant. While I've heard folks ask for messages to be slowed down, in the first step of a conversation speed is critical.

The fast response is feedback to the person texting that they have connected with your business properly. It alleviates any concerns the contact may have and helps them to complete the conversation as you desire.

If you do decide to send a MMS[18], do it after step one so as to not create unnecessary delays.

I really love to **end my conversations** in one of two ways: either with an **open-ended question** designed to elicit a conversation or with a link to a **survey/evaluation**.

Surveys and evaluations are great to help you determine an interest level, tailor follow-up specific to the needs and interests of the contact, direct thoughts and preparation for the buying decision.

Surveys can be very easy for the contact to go through. I cover how simple this can be in my chapter on *Strategies That Work.*

---

18 MMS is short for Multimedia Messaging Service. Carriers allow 1,600 characters of text and video, audio, vCards, and a few other formats to be sent as part of a MMS, however since it uses data, not everyone can receive them. That being said, data is included in most modern phone service contracts and shouldn't be an issue. Because an MMS is being sent through the data network, it limits media attachments to 500kb. That's a very short, low quality video or a decent image. You may have grown accustomed to sending large high quality videos via your messaging app and be confused as to why that works but won't with a MMS. It may be because you're using iMessage, which uses data and bypasses the carrier's MMS network. That's an enhancement by Apple or Android for their equivalent service.

MMS is a very powerful way to communicate. My favorite medias to use in text messaging are images, video, and vCard.

MMS Images

Images are a great way to:

- Introduce yourself
- Display a product
- Communicate a thousand words with a single image

With **dynamic images**, you can personalize that image in a way that will really capture the attention of the contact.

Here's a picture of my brother Trent holding a piece of paper. With the dynamic image I can overlay any text I want and include the contact's name. You better believe that gets attention.

I really love using images with text messages.

The added benefit to using MMS is when we attach any media to a text message, we go from a carrier set limit of 160 characters to a limit of 1,600 characters.

I don't recommend you add ten times the text to a message just because you've attached media, but knowing you can go a little bit longer than the standard 160 characters gives you a little more freedom to write your message the way that you would like to.

MMS vCard

My next favorite media to attach to a multimedia text message is the **vCard**.

This is the contact card that you have on your contacts list on your mobile phone. It's a great way to get your information in their phone. I'll share a strategy that's really powerful for doing this later on.

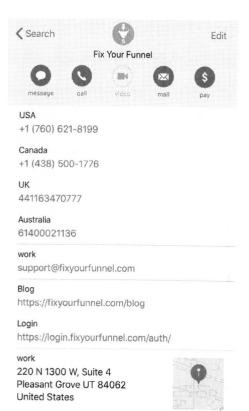

Another benefit of this is you get immediate recognition when you call or text because your logo or your face along with your company name will show up when you call or text them. This makes it easier for them to decide to answer the phone or respond to your text message.

This branding is very effective. When you send the emails, text messages, or make phone calls, your name or brand is going to be there[19].

This makes it easier and more convenient for them to re-call you, respond to you, and be happy to receive your messages in the future, assuming you're making continual deposits in their attention currency account.

MMS Video

The final media that I like to send with a multimedia text message is **video**.

Because of industry standards and carrier limitations with a text message, we can only send a short, low-quality video, but it's still a great opportunity to have a personal connection.

Even with a low quality video, you can communicate in a way that is unique and allows you to have tone

---

19 On this note, make sure you've set up all of your email addresses with Gravatar. Gravatar.com is used by most email service providers to place your logo or image next to your email address which can enhance your visibility in a tough place, the email inbox.

inflections, facial expressions, nonverbal language, and body language, all expressed through the video.

It can be very powerful, even if the video is short and low-quality.

Trackable Links

Sometimes there's more information than what you can get in a image, a vCard, or a low quality video that you'd like to send to a prospect via text message. This is where **links** come into play.

In the email dilemma chapter, I mentioned that the only metric that's really valuable is engagement. The same holds true for text messaging.

When people tap a link in a text message, you want to know that they actually took that action. It gives you a lot of information to work with to better customize your future communication with them when you know that they've actually tapped a link in a text message you sent.

You want to use trackable links. Be careful though, because if trackable links are too short, like bitly links, they can raise red flags with carriers because spammers tend to use short links like bitly links. In order to make sure your message gets delivered, I recommend you avoid short trackable links if you can.

The ideal is to use your own custom domain for trackable links. Trackable links are unique from standard links in that a unique link is created for each destination and contact. This unique link allows you to track that the link was tapped by the contact, but it also allows you to customize variables attached to the link that you can use to connect to deeper content.

This could be anything from a video that can be hosted on YouTube or on your own blog, to sales pages where you may communicate more information about what's going on with your offer to the market, to membership sites. There's a whole host of content you can link to.

What's really important is you want to keep the connection you have created. You've had people text in to you, you've collected some information, but that information is mostly associated with the mobile phone.

When you have people tap one of your trackable links, you want to keep that connection so you don't end up with multiple contact records for the same person in your CRM.

When moving a contact from a text message that is connected to the phone number to a page on your website where you might collect other information, like an address, make sure that you're maintaining that connection.[20]

You need to have some way of making sure that the data you collect on the website will be associated to the phone number in your client relationship management or marketing automation software. The solutions that I use for texting do this natively[21].

Messaging Follow-Up

While lead capture is important and very interesting, some of the most powerful use cases for text messaging happen in follow-up and conversion to sales.

As I engage in messaging follow-up, I focus on using something called a conversation starter.

A **conversation starter** is asking that open-ended question that will elicit a response from the contact. Any type of response will give us an opportunity to start to engage in a conversation.

When I'm crafting the perfect conversation starter question, I think about a few things.

---

20 When you're moving someone from one place to another on the internet there are a few ways to keep track of that person. One of the most reliable are query string variables in a URL. A query string is the collection of characters that follow a question mark in a URL. A URL is the web address of a page on the internet. It starts with http, includes your domain name and if there is a question mark in the URL, that means that a query string is present. Query strings may contain variables which are a collection of labels and values. These are separated by ampersands. I know this is technical, but if you were curious, now you know. ;)

21 Again, if you need recommendations on what texting platform to use, text my team at (949) 835-5300 and they'll ask a few questions to determine which one will be best for you.

- *Where is the contact at the time the message is being sent?*[22]

- *What have they learned that they probably didn't know?* If they interacted with a video link I sent them and I tracked that they watched that video[23], this creates the perfect opportunity for me to ask them a question about the content. Maybe they learned some new information and it would be appropriate for me to ask them if they have a question about it.

- *What would be a natural question that they may already be thinking about that you could ask to spark them to enter into a conversation?*

I use these three questions to help myself think through what my conversation starter should be that will be initiated by a campaign in my marketing automation software.

What's great about these conversation starters is they give you a real opportunity to treat people as people, to think about where they are in that journey of becoming a client or a customer, and help them to be able to get the answers to the questions that they may naturally have.

---

22 Here I don't mean where they are physically, but where are they mentally on the journey to becoming a customer?

23 Video tracking is a powerful part of the strategies I use when pushing a contact to a video. Consumption of a video gives me extremely valuable feedback that I can use to either improve my delivery in future videos, or, more importantly, judge how interested they are in what I've expressed. Higher lives of interest indicate it's time to start a conversation while lower consumption may indicate I should hold off on engaging in a conversation starter, or modify my conversation starter to address the lack of interest. Knowing when to ramp up or when to stop are both valuable.

When I'm doing follow up, I usually think about doing conversation starters, but sometimes I'm going to deliver content.

Delivering Content

In the example I mentioned before of using Facebook lead ads, the question we asked was, *"May we text this video to you immediately?"*

When they answer yes, I send out a text message with a **link to a longer video** where that person can get more information about what we can do to help them.

Another type of content you may deliver via text message is a **link to a PDF** or **to a Facebook group**.

Whatever you're delivering, text message can be the most effective way to do it because it skips all the junk that you can run into with email. As a result, your message is going to be seen and consumed much quicker and with higher reliability.

Reinforce an Email

Another great way I use text messaging in follow-up is to reference another action that I've taken with my marketing automation software. One place where I'll use this approach is when I send a critical email, because email is a better medium for the particular message, but I want to make sure that they see it.

After sending the email I'll send a text that says, *"Hey, Bill, I just sent you really important email, please check it out. Subject says READ NOW. -Ryan"*

I usually don't tell them what's in the email because I want to use a little bit of that curiosity in our nature to get them to take the action I want.

Reference a Voicemail

Another place where I'll use a text message to reference another action is after I've made a call. If I made a phone call and I end up getting voicemail, I'll send a text message saying, *"Bill, I just left you a voicemail, please listen to it. I look forward to hearing what you think."*

Mailed a Package

Finally, another place where I might reference actions is if I mailed a package. I'll use a text message to let people know that I've mailed them a package and they should keep their eye out for it. People love packages, and it's great to get a notification that something is coming your way.

Just knowing that something is being shipped to you builds anticipation, which can be a very positive emotion when topped off with a great delivery.

As important as text message lead capture is, and as important as automated text message follow-up is through marketing automation campaigns, the real power of text messaging is in *live texting*.

Live Texting

The most important texting you can do when it comes to mobile marketing is one-on-one texting with the prospect, especially when it's initiated by them.

When you're working with live texting, one of the things you really want to have is transparency for your entire team. If you are a solo-preneur, that's a lot easier. But, if you are working with a team of individuals and you want to have multiple layers of coverage in making sure that you respond to live text messages, then you want transparency in that text message communication.

Overlapping coverage, meaning more than one person will be notified of incoming text messages and can check for messages, is ideal. If you're busy and the other person can catch that conversation and respond to it, the customer is going to be happy that they received a timely response and you're not going to be running ragged because you're constantly on call.

You really want to allow automation to take care of being consistent with automated conversation starters, but when people respond to your automated conversation starters, your ability to respond with a human touch makes all the difference. In doing that, you preserve your humanity and focus your energy and attention not on being consistent, but on connecting with people.

Where you really shine as a person is in your ability to connect with other people, be empathetic, listen to what they're looking for, and help them get it.

So when you're using texting in your business you must have this capability. Anything short of live responses is a complete and total fail. Because of that, you also need to get push notifications to your smartphone.

The worst thing that can happen is for you to get text messages sent to your business that you don't even know about and you miss the opportunity to respond to the contact.

The lack of response creates a similar feel to social media pages for businesses or blogs that never respond to comments. It creates that feeling that these organizations are either out of business, or will be soon, because they don't care enough to respond.

You really want to make sure you have push notifications coming to your phone and that you can actually respond to messages straight from your phone or from your computer.

You are probably on your computer more frequently than you'd like to be, so it's important that your live texting solution allows you to text from your computer as well.

> *The ability to engage one-on-one with a prospect, to really communicate, is what will lead to more sales being closed in your business.*

If you have a successful business that's already closing sales and already doing well relying on email alone, you are in for a real treat.

One person we helped was a internet marketer named Frank Kern. He was running webinars to sell. But, like anybody that teaches through webinar, he discovered that not everybody that attended bought. He was selling well by anyone's standards, but he wanted to sell more.

Why didn't they buy?

This is probably true for you if you sell in this way, and the reason is, **they've got questions**! They have questions that they didn't feel comfortable asking in a group environment or that they didn't think to ask until after the webinar.

So, together with a fellow named Ross Walker, he implemented a quick strategy to send a text message after people had a chance to buy, but didn't.

Those people who attended his webinar but didn't buy received a text message (*Yes, they know* **Marketing Rule #19**, *so they captured the mobile phone number and permission to text during the webinar registration*) that said something like this: "*Hi, this is Aurora from Frank's office. He's running a marketing experiment with a special price, would you like to know more?*"

The result was he doubled his webinar sales.

I want to break down this example a bit because there is so much packed into the text message they went with.

First, the message clarifies that the text is being sent from a member of Frank's team and not Frank himself. That might seem like a bad thing, but the reality is that Frank isn't going to be responding to those text messages, so he didn't want to be deceptive.

Additionally, it positions Frank well as being a boss with team members who are working toward a common goal. He's a leader, not the front line worker.

If you've ever listened to Frank you'll know he's frequently running *marketing experiments*, so that phrase is part of his tribe's common language. People who have listened to him will immediately recognize it as being consistent. They also know that *marketing experiment* means better price in some way.

What's really interesting is that it is an indirect way to elicit a conversation that is particular to Frank's style. He knows that if the non-buyer was on the fence, but still interested, curiosity about the particulars of the marketing experiment will get them to reply.

While this exact approach won't work for everyone, the concept will. If you don't have all the fancy set up that Frank does, you could just text the attending non-buyer, *"I noticed you didn't invest in what I offered on the webinar. Do you mind if I ask you why? Thanks, Ryan."*

Not everyone you text will reply, but that's not really what you're looking for, is it? You just need those who were on the fence and haven't taken action yet.

By the way, Ross later told me that **Frank was *very* angry** that he had twice as many sales after he implemented the live texting into his process.

He wanted to sell to as many people as he could because *he knew he could help them*. The fact that half of the people that he had the potential to help left without getting his help infuriated him.

Live texting is so powerful that I really can't over state it enough, and this is just one example of how you can be using it to really connect with people and give them an opportunity to express their needs and, as a result, help more people be able to do business with you.

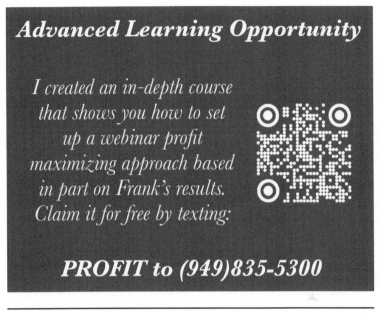

Advanced Learning Opportunity

I created an in-depth course that shows you how to set up a webinar profit maximizing approach based in part on Frank's results. Claim it for free by texting:

PROFIT to (949)835-5300

Pre-Call Text Message

When our company started using text messaging, we were calling leads that didn't convert on their own.

One day a sales person on our team said, *"Hey, I wonder what would happen if we sent a text message **before** we call them."*

I thought about that and said, *"Well, what the heck, let's give it a try."*

I mean, we had permission to text the people that were in our database, so it made sense for us to go ahead and send them a text before we called.

What occurred was phenomenal.

This salesperson **quadrupled** the number of people they talked to per call they made. If you've done outbound calls, then you know that the most common outcome of a outbound call is voicemail.

If you think about it, why is it that you get voicemail so often when you're calling? Some people, especially sales people, if they get in their heads, can think that the reason people aren't answering is because they don't want to talk to them.

The truth is further from that than you would believe.

The most common reason that people don't answer the phone is because because they're busy. A very close second is they don't recognize the number calling them. Is that true for you? I know it is for me.

If I don't recognize a number or I'm busy, I just don't answer. I don't have time to interrupt my flow with someone I don't know, calling me about I don't know what.

So you see, it has little to do with their level of interest in having the conversation with you. It has much more to do with the fact that they've got a lot going on in life and they're making decisions in order to preserve their time.

Frequently, that means they miss out on opportunities to talk with people they actually want to talk to who could really help them solve problems that they want solved or pursue dreams that they really want to fulfill.

When we started sending pre-call text messages to those people who we had already opened the door to send text messages to, we discovered something fascinating.

When we called people, they did one of four things.

1. Ignored the text but answered when we called.
2. Texted back to say that they were busy and scheduled a time for a call.
3. Texted back that they were not interested *(which was fantastic because the last thing you want is to call somebody 20 times who has no interest in talking to you)*
4. Didn't text back or answer the phone and we just left a voicemail.

No matter what, to know that for every 100 calls we made, we were going to talk to four times as many people made a dramatic difference in sales and the morale of the sales team.

In fact, we hear this quite frequently from people who use this strategy. Their sales people are suddenly invigorated with excitement because they're having more conversations with people who are actually interested in talking with them.

Sales are tough enough, but thinking that you're always the bad guy is even worse.

When you can give your sales team the opportunity to know that they're connecting with people who actually want to talk to them, which is what the pre-call text message does, it gets them excited about the opportunities that are before them and they start selling like never before.

Action Suggestions

Before you continue on, jot some quick notes in the margins of this book. Note the inspiration that came to you as you're reading. If some questions came to mind, jot those down too. Or, if you're really proactive, text my team at (949) 835-5300 with any questions that came up.

As I've observed my own progress and the traits of successful entrepreneurs I know, I've noticed a common characteristic: they get started **immediately** when inspiration hits.

Of course, no one can finish everything in an instant, but these people take immediate action when inspiration hits and map out a rough game plan for finishing the idea.

This approach creates momentum in life. Yes, some of the ideas are half baked when they first come out, but implementing the plan fleshes them out and either kills them or allows them to bear fruit.

Not every idea you get as you read this book will be a winner, that's life. However, enough of them will be that you'll be way better off for taking action instead of doing what you might have done in the past and saying, *"Yeah, that's a good idea. I'll do that tomorrow."*

When I was a young man living in Brazil, I met a 93 year old guy who started philosophizing with me and my friend. When we said we'd come back tomorrow and visit some more, he said, *"Tomorrow never comes."*

I immediately understood his message. Tomorrow is always a day away. Take some action **now**. That action, imperfect as it may be, breeds more action and creates momentum to take you to new places.

So if you haven't already, write down some of your ideas so you don't lose them, and as you read *Strategies That Work*, make sure you really mark up and write down what sticks out to you.

All this reminiscing on my time in Brazil has me thirsty for some Guarana.

Chapter 6

NEVER DO THIS

I hope by this point you're super excited to be incorporating text messaging into what you're doing in your marketing and sales. But before you do, I feel like it's critical that I share some bad examples so you can avoid some heartache and problems.

The reason I called this chapter **Never Do This** is because these are things that people do that are really stupid, even though I know in some cases they have good intentions.

Story #1

A company started a texting account, identified which numbers they had in their database that were mobile, and just started broadcasting promotional text messages in mass.

People complained and opted out, and that company ended up giving up on text messaging in their business and missed out on all that was possible.

What Went Wrong?

They didn't get permission in the first place, and they violated trust because those contacts didn't have any idea that they were going to be texted. Worse yet, they texted promotions. They were looking at the list like a bunch of money bags instead of people.

Doing things that your relationship isn't set up to do damages trust. This company hadn't opened the door for texting, so it wasn't an expectation in the relationship. Further they exhausted all attention currency, destroying the effectiveness of any other method of communication. See, damaged trust weakens relationships. Weakened relationships have no redeeming qualities.

In a worst-case scenario, it's possible this company could have experienced major legal trouble.

Maybe not, but either way, it's a dumb business move.

What Should Be Done?

If you're going to communicate with people, make sure it's in a context they expect because of the history that you've built with them.

If you have a list of people that you want to develop a relationship with and you want text messaging to be part of that communication relationship, you have to start asking for permission through the mediums that you've already established with them.

For example, if you have an email only list, then **ask for permission to text** in an email.

I wouldn't do this by just saying, *"Would you mind if I periodically sent you some important information in a text message?" (although you could)*, because this approach has a number of holes in it.

I would want to try to add some value and, as a part of adding that value, invite them to start texting with you. Getting them to initiate the texting opens the door in a more effective way than gathering their number any other way.

One thing to look out for is unifying their captured number with your contact record for them. This complication is an effect of not collecting the mobile phone number in the first place, but it's not impossible to overcome.

Use a keyword/phone number lead capture mechanism and gather an email address in the process. For some marketing automation systems[24], the

---

24 Since I've been working with marketing automation systems for over a decade as a developer, which means I get into the nitty gritty of how these systems work, I know the good, bad and ugly of many of them. The truth is, many of them will work fine, but what will limit your options is the availability of great messaging platforms that will extend marketing automation systems. Since the landscape of these software solutions is always changing, just text my team at (949) 835-5300 if you'd like a recommendation on what I recommend based on your needs and situation.

presence of an existing email address will cause an automatic merging of phone number and existing contact information.

Other systems may require a manual de-duplication process, but again, that's the downside of not collecting the right information at the right time.

Your lure to get them to text your keyword may be exclusive content (*like a special master class on the topic they are interested in or a special webinar*), a tip of the day for seven days, or some special way that they can get an inside track on information that would be valuable to them.

Don't promote, build relationships with texting.

Text messaging is very intimate. Texting occurs on a device that they carry with them all day long. You want to be respectful of that.

We have clearly established that text messages get way more attention than emails. So when you're texting, make sure you're not just asking them (*or I should say, telling them*) to do something that you want, but rather that you're enhancing their life in some way.

Remember to consider attention currency. This never goes out of style. It's always going to be a factor.

Even after you've acquired permission and you do send out a text message, make sure it's something that they have indicated that they want based on their previous interaction with your marketing.

Story #2

A company sent a text message after they left a voicemail. That's a good strategy. The problem is, they used the same text message every time.

Eventually, people opted out and carriers started blocking messages from that phone number.

What Went Wrong?

The user didn't think about what it's like to receive the same message every time. They didn't think about what the experience would be for the person on their list.

This means they were probably looking at the person as a moneybag and not as a real human being. The messages felt automated because they were all the same.

What Should Be Done?

They should have switched up the outgoing message at each point of contact where the text is being used. If there's no response coming from either the phone call and the voicemail left or the text message sent, dial back the texting.

Texting is really effective when there's a relationship going on, when there's communication happening. But when you're not getting any communication in return, dial it back.

If you started texting a friend and they were texting you and you were going back and forth and it was really great and then suddenly they stopped responding, *how many times would you text them?*

Would you text them every day?

Would you text them once an hour?

If you did, you wouldn't have much of a relationship going forward.

Be thoughtful.

Think about what you should be doing based on how you would text a friend or a relative that you like.

Story #3

A company had an auto reply to all incoming text messages that said that the company didn't respond to incoming text messages, telling people to email them or call them at a different number from the number that the contact was texting. In some outbound messages, they even appended, *"Do not reply. Responses not monitored."*

This ticked people off. They complained and they opted out. The carrier started to block messages.

What Went Wrong?

If you talk to somebody and you don't let them respond in the same way, it's rude. It's a basic form of societal politeness that we would let other people communicate back to us and not just talk **at** them. This lack of respect kills relationships.

Damaged Relationships Kill Sales

I call this out for those who struggle with making the right decision. If you are tempted to text at people because it will be cheaper, or easier in your head, realize that you're only setting yourself up for failure.

Even if it were cheaper and easier, which it isn't, in any way, shape or form, it damages relationship and people don't even buy cheap when the relationship is bad.

And if for some reason they do, I guarantee you don't want them as customers...no matter how desperate you may be at this moment for sales.

You need to make sure that if you're going to text somebody, they can text you back. Not doing so makes you look like an amateur. It shows that you're only interested in talking *at* or treating people like moneybags versus talking *with* and treating them like human beings.

What Should Be Done?

Always be ready to receive responses to text messages you sent out. Don't expect people to communicate in a different way than you're communicating with them at that moment.

You wouldn't call somebody on the phone, not listen to a word they say, just talk at them, and then say, *"Hey, if you want to respond, email me."*

You wouldn't send out an email and say *"Don't respond to this email because we don't check our inbox."*

If you do, there's probably something wrong in your business and let's hope that you can learn from what we're talking about here to fix it.

Make sure that you let people communicate with you in the way that you are trying to communicate with them.

That's just basic courtesy.

Story #4

A company bought a list of leads. This is always kind of a bad thing to do from my perspective, but then to make it worse, they texted them without permission.

On top of that, they didn't identify themselves either! They made the assumption that everybody knew who they were, even though there was no way that could have been possible.

They ticked people off and carriers began to block their text messages.

What Went Wrong?

You can't text people without their permission.

I think we've covered that enough, but you especially can't text people that have no relationship with you and expect to see good things happen.

No one wakes up in the morning and says, *"Boy, I sure hope someone **I don't know** texts me and **asks me to buy** something."*

Sure, if you try this approach you might get 1 out of 10,000 people that are glad you texted them, but it's not worth all the damage you caused.

And I'm not even talking about the potential legal ramifications. I believe that…

...whatever you put out comes back to you.

If you put out treating people like moneybags or objects, that's going to come back to you and it's not going to come back in a pleasant format.

Make sure that you're communicating with people as people.

Remember to identify yourself.

Even if you think you've got a good relationship with this contact, it's a good idea to mention who you are in every text message you send out so you can be certain that they identify your number with you.

There are strategies in this book that involve getting your contact information on your contact's phone. These can help in making sure that when you send a text message, they'll easily be able to identify that this text message came from you.

If you lead out a message identifying yourself, some smartphones will even suggest your name when you text, but that may lack the business context, so best to identify yourself.

Trent was working with a lady we'll call Debs. She was running a spa that she wanted to grow. Trent provided her with a strategy that directly addressed what they had identified as the biggest opportunity to grow by following the process I outline in my book, **How To Fix Your Funnel**.

The strategy was to have new spa clients text a key word to a number that would start a campaign that would check in with them after their treatment to make sure they were happy with it, and then invite them to reschedule a new appointment.

Since rescheduling was their biggest opportunity it made total sense.

Trent checked in a few weeks later and Debs said she hadn't implemented the strategy because the campaign wasn't tied into her spa scheduling software.

Her result: Same results as before…less than 20% reschedule rate.

What Went Wrong?

Debs made excuses for not taking action instead of just doing what needed to be done.

Admittedly, we may not have updated her map of the territory sufficiently, but when Trent left the initial meeting, Debs was excited! She knew that the strategy would make a difference, but she made a critical mistake.

She didn't take immediate action.

What Should Be Done?

When you identify a strategy that you know is focused on the right problem, you take action. Not taking action would be like my kids typing in a destination in the Honda Pilot after I bought the map update, and then not putting the car into drive.

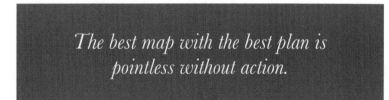

The best map with the best plan is pointless without action.

When you've identified a good strategy that will improve your profits, start **immediately**. Even if the plan will take a while to fully implement, starting immediately with any step you can take now will do more for your success than anything I know.

Debs also laid blame on an external situation to excuse her lack of action. You have to realize that blaming other things is a mechanism we humans use to relieve the pressure of guilt. Guilt is designed to point out to you that you're off course. It shouldn't be used to beat yourself up, but it also shouldn't be ignored or blamed away.

Blaming gives up your power to do something about your situation. I hope you noticed that while I was using Debs poor choices to explain her outcome, I also mentioned what my company can do better. That acknowledgement comes from a desire to be in integrity.

Integrity means to be whole. When we don't acknowledge what we are facing, we are modifying our map to match our wish of what the world would be. Be wary of that. Adding willful distortions to your map of the territory is a great way to get VERY lost. Willful distortions of your map splinters you as a person and, as a result, weakens you.

Story #6

We were working with a company that sold at free events. At the events they would pass out a piece of paper that asked the attendees a few questions about their experience and gathered their contact information.

Sales people would do this at meetings and then do nothing with the information gathered.

We set up a strategy to gather this information with an automated messaging conversation that fed a campaign that would follow up with the attendees based on the data gathered from the automated messaging conversation.

One of the things that the questions were designed to identify is which of the attendees would be willing and able to sponsor another free event.

The more events the sales person held, the more they sold. In fact, it was a known range of revenue that would be generated at the average event, so forecasting the value of an event was easy to do.

One of the sales people started calculating the cost of using texting instead of paper and decided to just use paper.

What Went Wrong?

The sales person fell for a classic mistake:

Tripping over dollars to pick up pennies.

The text messages would cost about $7 at the average event. The average event generated $500 in sales.

Human nature was causing the sales person to forget to use the information they collected on paper on a regular basis, so the number of events they were able to hold was stagnant.

Looking at cost without considering return on cost/ investment led to a poor choice that stifled results. Unfortunately as a business owner or sales person we don't all get the same education. While understanding the concept of ROI is a fundamental concept of business, not everyone has received the lesson.

What Should Be Done?

It's important to focus on the big picture and face reality. And, the reality is, the sales person wasn't acknowledging their human nature. Instead they pretended they were an angel who never forgets and always follows process. I don't think it's too harsh to call this naive.

Deal with the reality of human nature and do what is reasonable to mitigate it's impact on your profits. In this case, it means look carefully at the math of the business.

Spending $7 to eliminate human nature would identify and initiate a conversation with four more hosts than the paper method. Spending $7 generates $2,000 in sales.

That's a very good ROI. Besides the improved sales, it also would eliminate human action as the campaign, which is only set up once, does all the heavy lifting of gathering information, making sense of it, and following up appropriately with the contacts.

All the sales person has to do is focus on connecting with people and replying to incoming text messages in response to campaign initiated messages to contacts.

More Stories...

I tried to come up with more stupid things people do, but really that's about it. If you want to have a great experience with texting it's really simple:

Treat people like people.

Remember the Golden Rule. Do unto others as you would have others do unto you.

Look at people like moneybags and life will suck.

Look at them like people and the world is your oyster.

Don't send text messages when you haven't opened that door first.

Know your business' math so you can follow strategies based on ROI.

Start immediately and don't delay when you know what to do.

Remember Marketing Rule #19 and that there are no shortcuts in life.

I know people sometimes pursue shortcuts, usually out of desperation, and believe me, I've been in that desperate place before. I know what it's like to be tempted to take a shortcut, to try and get a quick win. But the reality is, it never works out.

You're going to be way better off to get some really solid strategies and apply them over and over again.

The simple mechanisms you've learned in the previous chapter and the ones that you will learn in the next chapter, if applied consistently and used reliably, will produce way better results for you than shortcuts and hacks.

Make sure that you don't fall into that trap. And if you're feeling desperate, if you're feeling overwhelmed, if you're feeling unsure, reach out to me - you've got my number.

I'm happy to help you because I've been there before. I *know* what it's like.

But if you read this book and you're thoughtful about it, I'm hoping that you'll be able to find a solution that doesn't involve doing the wrong thing in the wrong way.

Chapter 7

STRATEGIES THAT WORK

This is my favorite chapter in the book because, with these strategies, you'll see that really simple mechanisms can transform your business.

I use the term mechanisms because it implies a simple process. Over the years of building successful businesses and helping others do the same, simple has been a recurring theme.

There is a real tendency in marketing and sales to over complicate processes. I think it's simply because we can that so many do.

Marketing automation makes it possible to do almost anything you can think of, but my experience has been that the more complicated the marketing automation, the more likely it is that business will struggle in some way.

It could make money, but it will drive the people working it crazy.

In 1896, the Italian engineer and economist, Vilfredo Pareto noted that about 80% of Italy was owned by 20% of the population. That lead him to eventually discover the Pareto distribution, which would later be shortened to the 80-20 Rule by management consultant Joseph Juran.

I was turned on to the full implications of the Pareto distribution by Craig Jacobson a few years ago when he talked about it and its implications in business during a conference I was hosting in San Diego.

While the idea that 80% of your results will come from 20% of your effort has gained popularity, the truth is that Pareto discovered that there is a much 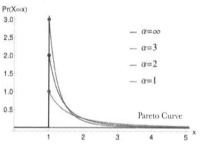 more fluid ratio that can be best summed up as the Pareto Curve, shown here.

You could say that 95% of your results will come from 5% of your efforts as accurately as you could say 80-20.

The big challenge is identifying which 5% of your efforts are producing the results. Well, this gets easier when your processes are simple and focused.

On the flip side, the more involved and complicated your marketing automation or sales processes are, the more difficult it will be to identify the 5% that is producing results.

If you really think about it, you know it to be true, so why is it so much more common for folks to brag about their complex campaigns than it is to even mention the simple ones?

Most of what gets in the way of the entrepreneur, blocking them from the results they seek, can be found between their own two ears.

There is some sense of value or validation that folks get from creating something complex and intricate. The fact that these complex automations never really produce results, or that they will break down within months of being put into production, doesn't seem to matter.

I frequently hear from business owners who have hired well known consultants to build out elaborate campaigns that never get used because no one in the business understands what they do.

I know that by saying this, many folks will be extremely ticked off to say the least. In some ways I've stabbed to the core, but if you can be totally open and look thoughtfully at your past successes, you'll find it's true.

So why all this philosophy before hard core strategy?

I need you to understand and accept the fact that simple mechanisms are the secret to your success.

Yes, you will have multiple mechanisms. But they will be laced together so clearly that you could draw it all out from memory for anyone at anytime.

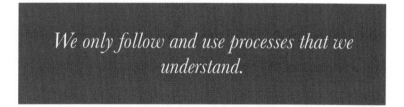

We only follow and use processes that we understand.

Maybe this philosophy just works for me because I have a simple mind. Maybe I'm just a minimalist at heart.

Yet, when you get these simple mechanisms that match up with your business model and your business needs and you put them into play, you'll discover they're not hard to maintain, they're easy to tweak, and they produce amazing results.

That's what I'm always looking for whenever I'm creating a mechanism, marketing campaign, or sales process in my business or the businesses of people that I work with.

You'll notice that with a lot of these strategies, I go more in depth on something that I mentioned briefly in a previous chapter. But I felt like it would be valuable to you for me to go into more detail on each of these specific strategies so you could pick up on the nuances and hopefully avoid some simple mistakes that might make them less effective.

Point Them in the Right Direction

Pointing a contact in the right direction is the process of sending a text message that refers to an important email you have sent the contact.

Use this technique judiciously.

Remember attention currency. Each time you send a text message that says, *"Hey, I just sent you an important email,"* it loses a little bit of its effectiveness, even if your email does deliver great value.

The natural inclination is to send the text message immediately after you send the email. But I recommend against this.

You should delay sending the text message by a couple hours after sending the email, or even longer if possible. You want to give the people who will actually see and engage with your email the chance to do so first *(remember, there are 5-25% of your list that are actually going to see, interact, and engage with that email)*.

If they engage with the email and I don't have to send a text to them, I saved myself a little bit of money and I didn't wear out my attention currency with that contact.

Send out the email and build a delay into your campaign so people that don't respond to the email will be able to get the text message.

To take this to the next level, include a short video telling them why they need to check that email. Make sure that the reason is one that talks to their motivations[25].

Direct Voicemail[26]

Sometimes I'll use a direct voice mail in this scenario as well. If you want to take it to yet another level, wait a couple hours after you send the email and after you've sent the text message to then send a direct voicemail message.

---

25 Way too often I see folks using what *they* want as the reason why a contact should take some behavior. It's amateurish and positions you poorly as someone who is needy. Needy people get spare change. It's just how things go. So instead, focus on what the contact is after as the reason for them to take the action you're prescribing.

26 Direct voicemail is a technique of delivering a voicemail message directly to the mobile phone inbox. I like it because not only is it your voice, with its ability to express so much more than text, available for them to hear, many modern smartphones transcribe the voicemail automatically, giving you yet another way for the message to be consumed.

A direct voice mail message costs more than a text message, but I'll use this when I've got something really important that I need contacts to see if they haven't responded to the email or the text message in an appropriate amount of time.

This will make it feel as though that message is super important. Of course, because I'm paying attention to the attention currency that I carry with that contact, I am going to be judicious about how I use the direct voicemail as well.

Note that because of the delay between each media that you use to deliver your message, you will reduce your overall financial *and* attention cost.

Another great unintended consequence of calling out an email with a text message or a direct voice mail is that email service providers are now using machine learning to monitor email engagement.

The more a contact engages with your emails, the better exposure it has in their email inbox. Likewise, if more of your contacts engage with your email using a particular email service provider then your emails will get better placement overall.

A decade ago, if you sent an email, it was only shown chronologically. Emails that were received sooner or later got better coverage depending on when the person checked their email inbox.

Today that's not so much the case. Machine learning is being used to prioritize emails that the email service provider determines, based on the user's behavior, are most important to them.

An email service provider's whole goal is to be able to provide the best experience possible for that user because if they provide a great experience for them, they'll keep them as a user. They use machine learning to create what they perceive to be a better experience for the contact, which is a plus if you can get people to engage with your emails and a major negative if you can't.

Another strong argument for paying attention to your *Attention Currency Account* with your contacts.

Pre-Call Text Message

I mentioned this briefly in an earlier chapter, but here I will go into more depth so you can execute this strategy effectively.

Identify yourself in the text you send.

This is contrary to what most people might think, but as we discussed earlier, people frequently don't answer phone calls because they don't know who's calling. You will not only identify who you are, but also why you're going to call.

This goes against every ounce of intuition that many salespeople have because they're afraid that if they announce *"Hi, Bill, this is Ryan from Fix Your Funnel. I'll be calling shortly to see if you have questions about how your business can using texting.,"* the person would never answer.

The truth is, the people who are going to buy need answers to their questions. When you tell them who you are and why you're calling, they're going to answer. If they can't answer, they're going to tell you when they can talk.

You definitely want to be telling people who you are and why you're going to be calling. This is what's going to help you to have the highest conversation rate[27] possible. I like to send the text message about 5-15 minutes before I call.

That heads-up is not only an act of courtesy[28], but it gives you the best chance that they will recognize, *"Oh, that's the person who just texted me,"* when you call.

---

[27] Conversation rate is a ratio of conversations you have to calls you initiate. After everything else, sales is a numbers game and the more conversations you have, the greater your potential to close sales is.

[28] https://youtu.be/Et--uvozgUM
Notice how much of a pain it is to type in a url vs a keyword and phone number. My editors wanted me to remove this and use a keyword instead, but I ended up vetoing that because I want to show how stupid it is to use a website url in print media. This video is really not that important and just mildly entertaining, so if you don't visit it, it won't be the end of the world.

Don't text if you aren't going to be calling.

I've had people who, when they start to use this strategy, send that pre-call text message to more people than they ended up calling. Don't do that, it makes you look unreliable, and reliability is very critical in business.

Don't send the text message unless you are *absolutely sure* you're going to call.

If you are, sending the pre-call text message is a great way to help a salesperson keep momentum.

As they send a text message, they're making a micro-commitment to themselves and the person they texted that they're going to make the call. If somebody is having a hard time making calls, this can help them a little bit by committing them to the call before they do it.

Be ready to receive responses.

You may be amazed at how many sales you end up closing through live text message conversations as a result of the pre-call text message. If a person is in a place where they can't receive a phone call, they may just text back their question and start the conversation that way.

We've heard many reports of people who end up closing way more sales than they thought they could just through text message conversations initiated by the pre-call text message.

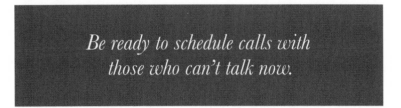

Be ready to schedule calls with those who can't talk now.

It's pretty interesting, but when someone knows who you are and why you're calling and they actually want to talk to you, they make sure to connect.

I like to use a calendaring system[29] to do this. It allows the sales person to give the contact a clear view of when the sales person is going to be available. Additionally, that means that you can automate reminders about that call for both the sales person and the contact so appointments are not missed.

That being said, it's pretty common for them to request that you call them in 30 minutes or in the afternoon. In those cases, don't over complicate the scheduling process. Just confirm you will and set a reminder.

---

29 Which one depends on the marketing automation system I'm using in the business. I recommend AppointmentCore or Calendly.

But if they want you to call some time other than today, you can ask them if there is a specific time that works for them and schedule it directly. If you run into more than one conflict, send a scheduling link from your calendaring system and make sure that if they don't schedule you reach out.

For scenarios like this I'll build alarms in to my automation that kick off if expected actions don't occur within a time frame I would expect.

Be prepared for a dramatic increase in conversations with your leads.

We've had people report going from 10% to 80% conversion as a result of having more conversations on the phone and by text message. Don't be too surprised when you see a dramatic increase in your sales conversions as a result of actually being able to have conversations.

Sales happen in conversations.

You have to have conversations in order to have sales.

This entire strategy hinges on the fact that you've opened the door to texting in the first place. If you try and do this same strategy with a group of people that have not opened the door for texting, you'll see the opposite effect. So, make sure you have that permission before you do anything.

Text Message Lead Capture from the Stage

This strategy is perhaps my favorite of all the strategies because it's one that can create a lot of momentum for your company.

Remember, I've had people go from only getting 10% of the room texting in to getting 110% as a result of following these guidelines, so pay close attention.

The strategy works if you're speaking to groups to sell or if you're just speaking to groups to generate interest.

Give the Audience Time

One thing that we discovered as we were doing our research on how people respond to the text message call to action is that it takes women about ten minutes to be able to see the keyword and phone number and then text into it.

That's not a sexist comment, this is simply because many women have a purse that they keep their phone in when they're paying attention to somebody speaking.

In order for you to make sure that you have plenty of time for everybody in the room to respond, you have to think about the person who may take the longest to get there.

When a text message call to action is presented to the audience, especially if you're doing a great job, they are going to be taking notes.

They'll need to complete the notes they're taking, then register what you're asking them to do.

They'll then have to discover where their phone is, and in the case of women, it may be in their purse. They've then got to dig through their purse to find their phone.

Then when they unlock their phone, they will have to get past any notifications on the home screen, open up the text messaging app, and start putting in the keyword and phone number.

This entire process can take about ten minutes.

As a result, you have to make sure that you're giving your audience plenty of time to be able to respond to your text message call to action. That ten minutes is assuming that they agree with the value of your call to action and that they're actually interested in the offer that you've made.

Because it can take time for people to decide if they want to take you up on your call to action, you should present the text message call to action *at least* ten minutes before the end of your presentation. Ideally you will **present your call to action for the first time in the first third** of your presentation.

After you've given the call to action and you need to move on to another slide, make sure that you move that call to action to the top of the remaining slides if you're presenting to a live audience. This will prevent the call to action from being blocked by someone's head.

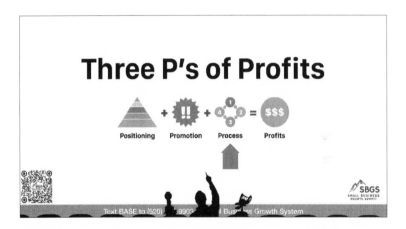

If you're putting a text message call to action on a webinar or some other presentation where there's no audience that could be in the way, then I would move the call to action to the bottom of the slides.

When you present the call to action the first time, you need to clearly state what they're going to get for texting in the keyword to your phone number.

Make sure they understand how they are going to benefit by taking action, then walk them through what will happen when they text the keyword to your number.

Say my text message conversation asks them for their name, then for their email.

I would say, *"When you text PROFIT to 949-835-5300, I'm going to ask for your name, and then for your email address, and then I'm going to deliver a PDF to your email address with all the slides that you've been seeing today. I don't want you to worry about taking copious notes. Be present. Let your mind explore what we're going to be talking about and know that I'm going to be sending you all of my slides when you text in PROFIT to 949-835-5300."*

I walked the audience through exactly what they were going to get and what was going to happen so that they knew exactly what to expect.

When you are creating your automated messaging conversation, if the audience is under 500 people, you'll ask for name, then email address.

The reason for the 500 person cut off is because of the only real downside of a normal phone number: the rate of messages it can send per second. Since it is limited to one text message per second, if all 500 people texted in at once, the number would be throttled to respond back and it will take 500 seconds, or 8 minutes and 20 seconds.

That delay for a response would be pushing it for me. I want the initial response to be zippy. This is another reason to present your text message call to action early.

It takes time for some people to trust you enough to text in, but others will be on the same page with you from the first word. By noting when the first text message came in, you can get a feel for who was most in sync with you compared to those you had to win over.

Both are valuable, but the order does tell you something about the contact.

The added benefit of the distributed nature of their texting in is that it will create a natural buffer of demand on your number, and as a result provide a quicker experience for all attendees.

When you're speaking to a room greater than 500, I will skip the name step and just ask for the email address. I'll also make sure that the amount of time that the contact will be in the automated conversation once they text in the keyword will be a couple of days.

It's not uncommon for some members of very large audiences to text in the keyword *(which accomplishes 90% of what we hope the automated messaging conversation will do)* and wait until after the presentation to complete the conversation.

If they don't complete the next step, I will set up an alarm in my campaign to send a text message after the presentation is over to prompt them to complete what they started. This makes sure that I get what I need from them to keep the promise I made.

In certain extreme cases I won't even ask for the email address. If the audience is sufficiently large, I'll simply deliver the promised goods with a link to my website.

The final message of an automated messaging conversation should include one of two things:

- An open-ended question, one that will elicit some sort of response from them so you can have either you or your team engaged in a conversation with them
- A link to a survey or assessment.

I had one client who utilized the open-ended question during a presentation and actually had their team members sitting in the back of the room so they were fully aware of the context of each of the questions and comments that were coming from the audience.

They were responding to the audience's questions in real time, and the crowd was *mesmerized*. The speaker also had the incoming questions popping up on an iPad in front of him so he could address anything he thought would be valuable to the entire crowd.

They couldn't believe that they could have that kind of dynamic interaction with the speaker and, as a result, it was a wildly successful session for that speaker in terms of revenue and connection with people.

Autopilot Appointment Funnel

This is the process that Trent developed for that little business that collected over 70,000 leads. This strategy is designed for interruption-based marketing in Facebook and Instagram.

If you're marketing on Facebook or Instagram, you're going to want to pay close attention to this strategy. It is a game changer. I can't do it justice in words.

It starts with an ad on Facebook or Instagram connected to a Facebook lead ad that asks for:

- Full name
- Email address
- Phone number
- Permission[30] to text a link to a video that will give more details about what was offered in the ad.

---

30 Request Trent's master class to get the exact wording that he worked out over the course of generating 70K leads using this method. We sell this class for $500, which is a bargain because once you understand it and put it into play, its value is incalculable. But getting it for free is something I was glad Trent agreed to do for this book.

That information then gets pushed into the marketing automation software which then triggers a text message to the new lead with a link to the video, for those who gave us permission to text them, and an email to all the leads.

I know this kind of violates the attention currency rule by sending an email and a text, but because we're delivering on a promise we made in marketing, I want to make sure that they absolutely got the message. You use email as a backup and, if they give you permission, text as the primary.

The video is designed to communicate the offer with an invitation to talk to a sales rep about their specific situation. You can call them a sales rep or something else, but the call to action in the video is to talk to a real person about their specific situation.

There's so much power in this concept of telling people what it is that you can do for them and then saying, *"Let's check and see if this will work for you. Let's schedule a time for you to talk to a member of our team about your specific situation and needs and we'll evaluate if we are a match for you at this time."*

We use scheduling software to allow the contact to schedule a specific time to talk with our sales rep. Before the lead's scheduled appointment, we would send a text message reminder.

If we were having them call in, we would say, *"Just call me at (949) 835-5300 at 10:15am Mountain."*

That text message reminder is critical for helping them to make sure that life doesn't get in the way. It's *our* responsibility when we are trying to have a sales call to make sure that they remember to join us on the call.

Trent created a master class on this strategy and because you have this book, you can access it for free if you text:

FUNNEL to **(949) 835-5300**

When we initially started this particular business, we didn't have the Autopilot Appointment Funnel in place. We were doing ads and sending people to a video and we had six sales guys calling the leads.

When we switched to the Autopilot Appointment Funnel, we went from having six salespeople to one salesperson who was talking to people all day long and selling twice as much as six salespeople were when pounding the phones.

I've seen this strategy implemented multiple times in a wide variety of businesses and even business models and it never ceases to amaze me with the results it produces.

Trade Show Lead Capture

Trade shows are all about capturing leads.

While you can just collect business cards and use the Getting Your Name in Their Phone strategy, there's another approach that can improve your positioning with prospects as they come by the booth.

You print a large QR code with a keyword and phone number printed below it. When people come to the booth, you can engage with them by asking them to pull out their phone in order to get whatever your trade show offer is.

Todd, one of my 8 brothers, manning a booth using the Trade Show Lead Capture strategy.

You tailor the offer to match the audience, but let's say that we are giving a special resource.

Start by asking, *"Do you have an iPhone or Android?"*

This is a very interesting question because it usually has nothing to do with the offer and is very easy to answer. When the person answers, *huzzah!* They've engaged in a conversation and it's yours for the directing.

It's called the **Foot in the Door technique**.

Next ask them to point their camera at the QR code. If they have an iPhone, with a couple taps you can get them to text in the keyword and phone number because that QR code has the number and the keyword baked into it and it will automatically pre-fill their phone's messaging app with both the keyword and the phone number.

If they happen to have an Android phone that doesn't support QR codes, then you get them to open their text messaging app and type in the keyword and the phone number and boom, they're in your database and they've started on the customer journey with you.

When I shared this strategy that we've been using at trade shows with a gentleman that specializes in just helping companies get their trade shows working well, he was blown away and super excited to implement the same strategy with his clients.

Try it out and you'll be pleasantly surprised!

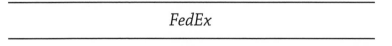

FedEx

When you absolutely must deliver something to someone, then text message is the way to go. You can use this when you have a critical video that needs to be delivered and consumed before the contact makes a buying decision.

Send a text message with a trackable link to the video. Track the click to the video and then track how much of the video is watched. Especially track if they watched the video to a critical point[31]. Set alarms for follow-up that should happen based on how far through the critical process the contact progressed.

If you send out the text and they never clicked the link, set an alarm to back up that process. Maybe it's a phone call, maybe it's another text or an email. Maybe it's a direct voice mail that goes out to make sure they didn't miss the text with a critical link.

If they tap the link to the video but they don't watch to the critical point, encourage them by letting them know that they have missed out on something really important to helping them get what they are after.

If they do watch the video to that critical point, you know the potential thought process they are going through. You can contact them on the phone or via

---

31 Every video ought to have a point. Here I'm calling that point the critical point. It's where you've made an argument or expressed an idea that if your prospect understands it, they are better prepared to make the best possible buying decision. That's why video tracking is so critical. You need to have the fact that they watched that moment feeding back into your marketing automation software so you can trigger the next step.

text message and ask them if they're ready to make that buying decision from that context.

I use these indications of action engagement to up the ante on how much I'm willing to invest into that next step of the relationship. If they go through that whole process and get to the video and watch it, maybe that's the point at which I engage a member of my team to make a phone call.

Regardless, when I absolutely have to get some piece of information delivered, I'm doing it with a text.

Creating a Personal Connection

I once opted into a company's lead capture on Facebook and the first text they sent me *(after getting my permission)* was a picture of the person who would be calling me and a message that they would be calling.

I was blown away.

I immediately felt much more open to receiving their call because they had created a personal connection. It increased my trust level even though I had no experience with them.

What was really interesting about the picture was it was not overly professional. They were dressed nicely, but it was a photo taken by their webcam at their desk.

It didn't give a feel of being too slick, but it was still nice.

As it turned out, they were a client! I was so excited to learn that they were using the techniques that I had taught and even taken them a step further.

Once I had that experience, I started teaching the same process to other people and using it in our own business.

When you send out a welcome text or an initial text to a person, include a photo of you or the member of your team that will interact with the customer and prospect. If you want to take this to the next level, use a dynamic image instead of a static image.

A dynamic image could have a picture of a member of your team holding a blank piece of paper, and over that piece of paper the dynamic image could insert their name and a phrase like, *"I'm excited to talk to you soon."*

Imagine your name being embedded on the image texted to you.

Not only do we have the personal connection of seeing the face of somebody that you will soon interact with, but a personalized message on the image is being sent to me and being sent so quickly or timed in a certain way that it feels very personal.

If you wanted to take this technique to yet another level, instead of the image, you could send a 15-30 second video introducing yourself and saying that you're looking forward to talking with them soon.

This is a great way to really put a face with the name and help people to know who they're going to be doing business with.

People do business with people.

Even if you've got a face for radio, a personal connection really does increase loyalty and trust, so don't be shy.

Besides all that, *nobody does this,* which helps you show up like no one else.

Showing up like nobody else can make a huge impression and gives you a lot of leeway as you get this new relationship off the ground.

Getting Your Name in their Phone

This can work with the personal connection strategy I just mentioned. All you have to do is add a vCard and ask them to add it to their contacts so they can reach you at any time by email, text, or phone.

In your contact card or vCard, make sure you include:

- Your logo or your face
- Your address if you are a local business
- All of your phone numbers that you may use
- All of your email addresses that you may use for you or your team members.

Then, when you call, email, or text them, your name and image will show up, increasing connection.

If you're going to use a vCard in an automated messaging conversation, include it on one of the last steps.

Priming the Pump

When you're delivering content through a text message, attach a video to prime the pump.

We now understand it's going to be low-quality and short, but explain in that video what they'll find when they tap the link that's included with the text message.

You can alternatively tell them what to do with the content provided, or just thank them for requesting it.

Let them know that if any questions come up as they go through the content, they can just text you.

This is a super effective way to make sure that the text you're sending is understood by the person receiving it and they know exactly what to do with it, or just to form that personal connection.

Business Card to Connection

In the Trade Show Lead Capture strategy, I mentioned that if you elect to just collect business cards there would be a strategy coming up. It has arrived.

It doesn't really matter how you receive the business card. This strategy can work equally well if you:

• Collect business cards at a trade show booth
• Get a card at a networking event
• Get a card at a social function

Take that business card and add the mobile phone and name into your marketing automation software. Next trigger a connection campaign[32].

Have that connection campaign send an immediate text with your vCard and, as a bonus, a video saying it was great to meet them.

You don't have to create a separate video for each and every person you meet. In fact, that would be the opposite of what we want to do because it wouldn't be scalable, reliable, or consistent.

Instead, do a generic video that is recorded with you thinking about a specific person, even though you may not mention them. Then, attach that to the text message that also has your vCard.

Let them know it was great to meet them and you look forward to staying in contact, that you've attached your vCard and you hope that they will add it to their phone and let you know if they ever have any questions that come up.

That in and of itself will make a great impression on people, but to take this to the next level we want to use an advanced connection campaign.

---

32 A connection campaign is one that is designed to reach out to a new contact and introduce yourself and/or your company and provide your contact information so that you can easily connect in the future. That's a very basic version. More advanced versions are mentioned above. If you are getting lost with the references to triggering campaigns and such, text or call my number (949) 835-5300 and we'll point you in the right direction.

It's called advanced because after sending the initial text with the vCard and video, it forks down one of three paths.

What determines which path the campaign will follow is how you mark the contact when the card is input into your marketing automation platform.

I use a 3 grade system. **A**, **B** and **C**.

A means that I really need to stay in contact with this person. So that leg of the campaign will send a unique text message each month with a conversation starter.

B means that I feel I should keep in periodic contact with this person. That leg of the campaign will send a unique text message each quarter with a conversation starter. It's a great idea to pick 4 messages from the 12 you create for **A** contacts.

C means that I feel I should check in with this contact annually, maybe as a courtesy. In that case, I'm sending a text message once a year. I usually queue up 4, and again, it can be the same 4 I selected for **B** contacts.

Some cards might not merit a letter grade at all. That's life.

What's beautiful about this is when those messages go out and the contact responds, you'll be notified on your mobile phone and be able to pick up those conversations and connect again.

This is a really powerful example of how you can mitigate your human nature and unreliability out of the equation and allow yourself to focus on connecting with people.

It's effective, very easy to do, and will set you apart from the crowd because most people aren't consistent and don't connect.

Digital Business Card

Business cards are great. But digital business cards are even better because they can be delivered and distributed freely and at virtually no cost. And, when they are accepted, they have a much longer life than a paper one.

A digital business card is really just a vCard, but I wanted to call them a digital business card so you think about them a little differently. When you do think of them like business cards, then maybe you'll send them more frequently with your text messages.

Magical Traveling Lead Capture

I recently got a Tesla Model 3 and besides the instant torque when I press on the accelerator, I love the simplicity of the machine.

There are hardly any moving parts, so its reliability and the low cost of maintenance is unmatched.

I want you to remember two things:

1. DEMO
2. (949) 835-5300

OK, do you have that memorized?

Fantastic! You just memorized a Magical Traveling Lead Capture!

It's simple and easy to remember and now it can go with you anywhere in the world!

You don't need a developer or designer. You just need to know when to invite a prospect to text your keyword to your number.

And because it's so easy, guess who else can remember it? Your prospects and your evangelists. When they run into someone who needs what you have, they will tell them to text your keyword.

I recommend you keep that keyword and phone number in your vCard as well.

Whenever I record a video, I include my main[33] keyword and phone number as a call to action.

---

33 It's important to have a main way that you generate leads. I'm all about testing different lead capture offers, but at all times have at least one that is your main, go-to call to action.

When I'm posting to any social network and I think a call to action is appropriate, I drop it in.

When I'm writing a blog post…I add it in.

When I get an unexpected chance to promote my business…I add it in.

When I'm creating a direct mail piece or a book…I add it in!

It truly is magical. It has few moving parts. It's easy to maintain. If I ever want to change up the conversation flow, I can. The keyword and number don't change.

Triple Touch Technique

Trent developed this strategy in his work with businesses needing help with their sales processes.

When you call somebody and you get a voicemail, have your automation send a unique text message and a unique email.

Once you've left the voicemail (*touch number one*), texted them (*touch number two*), and emailed them (*touch number three*), there's a really good chance they're going to know that you tried to reach them.

While most people do prefer text messaging, there are some that prefer phone calls and others, email. The

Triple Touch will make sure they can communicate with you in the way that best matches their preference.

Make sure you word your emails and text messages as you would if you wrote them to a **single person** in the event that you got their voicemail when you're calling them.

Again, when you think about automation, always think about an individual person in a unique one-to-one connection. If you do, then your messages will be more personal and more effective.

This technique can consume a lot of attention currency, so use it wisely. I wouldn't do this every time I left a voicemail, but sprinkled in, it can be very effective.

Text Nurture Campaign

This technique is really a variation on the Business Card to Connection technique, but I wanted it isolated on its own specifically because it doesn't have to be used just in conjunction with a business card.

We had some folks that were speaking at conferences once or twice a year. After the event, and after they captured hundreds of mobile phone numbers, they would put their texting account on hold until the next event.

For a whole year, they wouldn't text with their prospects that they had just captured from speaking on the stage with an automated text message conversation.

I'm pretty sure they thought they were saving money. But, they weren't. They were losing money and losing it big time.

We recommended that they incorporate an open ended question into their lead capture conversation. Then we helped them lace in text messages as part of their nurture sequence.

You've read this far, what do you think will be the result? Is it possible they will make more money than they were saving by continuing to engage their prospects in the medium that they captured the lead in?

Maybe they thought that since their customers bought on their own from emails, texting would be a waste. The best opportunities I find in email-only businesses lay in starting conversations with those people who did not buy, but should have.

If you take a look at the example of Frank Kern I mentioned before, he was already selling about a million dollars a year through his webinar process, but he was missing out on an additional million because he wasn't reaching out with a single text message to those who, by all accounts, should have bought on their own.

Understand that even if you're doing great without engaging prospects in conversation, if you start reaching out with a single text to those who should have bought, you may find that you have another half of your business hiding right under your nose.

Simple Surveys

I really want to make sure that you learn about surveys. I did mention them casually earlier in the book, but I feel like it's worth going into deeply.

Simple surveys are one of the most powerful tools you can use to prepare the mind of a prospect for the buying decision.

Powerful surveys have two basic components.

The first question in a survey is used to **separate contacts into logical groups**. These logical groups are those that represent the main needs or reasons that a prospect might buy from you. This will allow you to tailor your follow up communication to their needs.

The more tailored your communication is, the greater the perceived value from the contact's perspective. And the higher the perceived value, the more Attention Currency you'll bank with them.

You want the answers to your first question to break prospects up into three or four groups. Because of that, make the answers multiple choice. More than four groups and the tailoring of the follow up gets unmanageable.

That first question in your survey is going to accomplish a lot.

The reason I make it the first question of the survey is because I don't have any guarantees that people are going to complete the survey. I want the most important information gathered first, which is why I do the separation into different groups first.

The remaining three to five questions *(and I don't like to go for six questions in a simple survey)* are designed to **help them see the world differently**.

Sales is a process of exposing people to a whole new world, changing their paradigm, reframing the way that they see the world so they can make a better buying decision going forward.

We think in questions, so the right question can have a profound impact on our view of the world. But when somebody asks us a question, that by itself is not enough to impact our view.

What impacts our thinking is when we have to consider the question and evaluate our answer. When we consider a question, our mental guard allows the question to slip past it and enter into our great subconscious, where our values and beliefs live.

Once a question has slipped past the guard, it now has a chance to impact perspective and paradigm. So, be thoughtful about the questions you choose. Honestly, the answers don't matter nearly as much as the question.

I can't say I always include the best questions in my surveys. Sometimes I get lazy and just include one so I can learn a preference or desire, and not to modify their world view. But that's OK too.

You should be aware of the power of questions in simple surveys.

I prefer to use multiple choice answers in my surveys for a couple of reasons.

First, it simplifies the process of the person answering the question. Typing out an answer on a smartphone is a lot more work than tapping a button. Also, I know my topic, so I generally know what answers they're going to come up with. I can put those answers in front of them and let them decide which one best matches their scenario.

The other reason I use multiple choice answers is because it standardizes the answers and makes it easier for automation and personalization to occur as a result.

If creating a 4-6 question survey with multiple choice answers feels intimidating, remember that you don't have to create a bunch of them. In fact, in most cases I'd recommend creating just one survey that could be used in multiple situations.

You already know that I prefer to have one major lead capture keyword and number, and having your main or only survey attached to that automated conversation as part of the final step is a great way to go.

The survey solution I use also tracks their progress back to my marketing automation platform allowing me to use that progress as another signal of interest and as a result informing future communication decisions.

Customer Satisfaction Check-in to Referral Request

This is the final strategy I want to share with you, which is by no means the final strategy or way to use mobile marketing to radically transform your company.

Your reputation is your most valuable asset.

How people perceive your company can either cost you a ton of money or make you a ton of money. It really depends on what they think about you.

So, it's important that when you're delivering on the promises you make during marketing and sales you make sure your customer is happy about doing business with you.

Most businesses don't do this. I don't know if they just hope that customers are happy or they don't want to find out, but it's a big mistake to not be the first line of communication with your customers about their experience with you.

If you don't proactively seek out their feedback, they will probably deliver it in the way that they think is best. That could be Yelp, Google, a blog post, or a social media post. None of those are where you want complaints or dissatisfaction publicly displayed.

Ideally you want to ask them about their experience first.

One way to do that is to send a text message to check in with your customer at a point at which they should be able to tell you how satisfied they are with their experience.

If the experience has not been good, you have a perfect opportunity to fix it.

If they respond that it's been amazing, that's the perfect time to ask for a referral.

To execute this strategy, just set up an automated outbound text message to check in with the customer's experience at a point at which you believe that they have received what you promised. This will protect your reputation by giving you a chance to step in front of them tweeting out a negative comment about your company or leaving a bad review.

This instead gives you a chance to make things right or discover who is thrilled to death and give them an opportunity to refer you to somebody who can use your product or service.

This may seem like a simple little mechanism, but as I said before, the simplest mechanisms are often the most powerful in revolutionizing your business.

The Hidden Strategy

Hidden in between these various strategies and the chapter on new school texting were a lot of nuances. You may have picked up something that I did not write. You may have come up with an idea sparked by something I wrote but didn't explicitly say.

I hope that was the case because there are many other ways that people are using texting to effectively communicate and engage prospects and customers and, as a result, dramatically increase their bottom line revenue and profits.

If you did come up with a cool way to use text messaging that I did not explicitly layout in this book, I would love to hear about it, just text me: (949) 835-5300. I'm a constant student.

I love to learn and I love to learn from other small business owners as they use effective techniques to create deeper relationships and more revenue for their companies.

Epilogue

FOCUS ON THE LONG PLAY

In the movie **Now You See Me Two,** a set of magicians perform what is known as the *long play*.

The long play is laying out a trick that starts at the beginning of the show but is tied back in at the very end. The longer the performer takes to tie the trick back in to the performance, the greater the payoff.

The long play is almost always worth it, but the challenge of the long play, when it comes to business, is ***cash flow***[34].

In business, the long play is one of the best ways to do marketing. The problem is that most people, because of cash flow, don't feel like they can afford to work the

---

34 I was once teaching a bunch of teenage boys about business and I asked them why businesses fail. Poor idea! Bad management! Low prices! I agreed that all of these could be bad for business, then referenced successful businesses that had each one of these items. I then let them in on the secret: CASH FLOW. I don't know what kind of impact that made on those young men, but every time I run into one of the adults that was there he repeats that line. He knows exactly what I'm talking about too because he's been floating an exciting, but pioneering, business for some time, so he knows of what he speaks. Let cash flow dry up and you're toast. Keep cash flow good long enough and you'll probably learn how to mitigate any weaknesses in you or the business.

long play. They always keep their focus on the here and now…the short term.

If you are just focused on today only, chances are you're not making good decisions for your company.

I recently heard a CEO say, *"What I really think about each morning is, how can I push the company forward today?"*

This is a terrible perspective.

You have to keep the long play in mind.

The good news is, you can afford to start playing the long play now. There's something that you are doing *right now* that you don't need to be doing, and really shouldn't be doing. It's true for all of us.

Even if you think, *"I'm totally swamped, I'm totally busy, there's no way I could work the long play in my business,"* chances are there's something you're doing right now that you can drop from your life.

The truth is, whatever you've been doing to get the results you're getting today doesn't take up 100% of your time, I promise you.

As I said earlier, in automation there are 5% of the actions that are producing 95% of the results. Likewise, some small number of things that you're doing now are actually producing almost of your results, which means that you have a space in your effort that can be utilized for the long play.

I would like to encourage you to start asking yourself, *"How can I start working the long play as I continue to work my short-term hustle to get whatever needs to be done, done?"*

This is the difference between someone like Warren Buffet, who runs Berkshire Hathaway, and the way that he invests, versus the guy that's doing minute trades on the e-minis in his basement.

The guy that's doing the mini trades has to be right, and if he's not right he pays very quickly. With someone like Warren Buffet and what he does with his investing, it's always the long play. He may be wrong in the short term, but in the long term he's able to win.

The long play is much easier and more forgiving than the short-term hustle. You can start working the long play **now**. It may not pay off for a little bit, but you can start building it now.

> **You can't build the long play later.**

You have to start building it now. Once you get it in place, then it starts to pay off.

There are a few steps that you need to take to work the long play in marketing.

First off, **be clear on your message**.

What is it that you bring that is unique to the marketplace that will allow you to craft a compelling message?

To find your message, you always have to start with your customer.

What is it that your customer really needs and wants that they *think*[35] that your product or service can give them[36]?

What are you helping them accomplish?

Second, once you get that message down, **begin to publish your message**. How?

In terms of power for positioning, publishing a book is the most powerful media for you. With today's technology, you don't need anyone's permission to publish a book.

The next move is to find some existing authority, blog, periodical, or podcast.

---

35 Remember that what your prospect thinks is way more important that what you think. So always come at messaging from their perspective. This doesn't mean we won't be working to modify their perspective. That's exactly what marketing and sales are meant to do. But you must start from where they are and lead them to where they need to go in order to help them make the best buying decision.

36 No one wants what your business offers. They want what they believe it will give them. That's a critical distinction.

Find resources that are already out there, that already have your audience and are not competing with you. That's a great place to also get your message out.

This can be a little tougher because you need someone else to decide to promote your content. If you can't get that initially, don't sweat it. But if you can ride the coat tails of someone who already has your audience by adding value to their audience and making them look smart, do it!

Another way to establish a long play relationship is to create your own blog or podcast, Facebook page, and Twitter feed.

Bottom line, you have to get your message out there. The more you get your message out there, the better you're going to be able to work the long play.

Once you have your message out there, you are going to need to **pay to promote your best messages**.

You don't know for sure which message is going to resonate until you put it out there.

With a little bit of trial and error, you can find out what's getting response and attention organically.

Once you figure out what is working, you want to pay to promote it.

Finally, once folks are interacting with your messages, promote an *identifying*[37] call to action.

If I get somebody to go to my blog to interact with my content, whether it's a podcast, a video, or something else, then at that point, I can identify them on ad networks like Facebook or Google and then promote a call to action to them.

I don't usually drive folks to a hard call to action on the first time that I drive traffic somewhere because I'm going for the long play.

I want to give people an opportunity to interact with me and determine if we have a possible future relationship and that comes from me demonstrating my understanding of what they need.

Once I do that, then I'm in a position to be able to invite them to take the next action, which is to identify themselves. That's why I called it an *identifying* call to action.

Once you have identified a prospect, then you **invite them to become a customer**.

After they become customers, **invite them to become bigger and more frequent customers**.

---

37 Identifying Call to Action is a call to action that gathers some contact information, thereby identifying the prospect. This is to distinguish from the Marking Call to Action which is used to tag, pixel or mark a contact for remarketing. If you're dependent and only focused on the short term hustle, then you must drive traffic to Identifying Call to Actions only. The unique characteristic of the long play is the Marking Call to Action.

And then, finally, you **keep customers** and **help them to refer**.

That is the long play.

> *The long play requires persistence.*

But, it also builds *deeper relationships*. The quality of your customers will be much higher when you work the long play than if you only focus on the short term hustle. Just know that.

You might have to focus on the short term hustle to keep yourself above water, that's fine. But the long play is where you're going to build a business…something that's going to last for a long time and not flash in the pan.

Believe me, for all the effort you're going to put forth for a flash in the pan, you might as well put it into a long-term business.

> **The long play is also an investment in others.**

Let me share an example of the long play I mentioned to you before and how you make an investment in others that will pay off for you.

Our initial company, the one that we took from 0 to 1.3 million the first 12 months, had a very high profit margin.

We trained 40,000 people for three hours in person, in their city, on our dime. We did not charge them a penny to give them this education and the education was very good.

It was so good, in fact, that we had people come back 9, 10, 11 times, and not buy anything from us because they got so much out of the education and what we were giving to them.

So we trained over 40,000 people to find 3,000 customers.

What really matters is the math of the business.

Now, if teaching 40,000 to find 3,000 doesn't seem like good odds to you, realize that it really doesn't matter what the numbers are in terms of raw number of people that you're interacting with, it's the result that matters.

The math of our business allowed us to be able to train those 40,000 people, give them a ton of value, a ton of great education and only find 3,000 that were willing to become customers, and still win.

Here's how valuable those 3,000 people were to our business: After we stopped selling and training new people, our existing customers paid us $4,000,000 in recurring revenue to continue to support them.

While our competitors who had all focused on the short term hustle were going out of business, we were doing great.

Today I invest time to teach business marketing concepts and pay to put that free education in front of tens of thousands to find those who will become our customers, and I'm totally happy to do that. My other books are for sale on Amazon for $5, not because they are worthless, but because I want anyone who needs the education to get it. And I'm always working the long play.

I don't even sweat over the people who don't become customers, and hopefully I am helping them on their journey through business.

I'm totally pleased to do that, and you should be too. That's part of the long play.

Part of the long play is you don't look at everybody as a money bag, but you look at them as humans, people on this planet trying to get to achieve something. Something you can help them achieve.

Some of those people will see value in interacting with you in an exchange of money, and they'll become customers. If you see them like we do, they will become part of your family.

The long play is methodical.

If you've done the work to find out what you really need to be talking about in the first place, you'll be on a solid foundation.

Keep Moving Forward...

Made in the USA
Columbia, SC
16 February 2019